MAYA ETHNOLINGUISTIC IDENTITY

violence, cultural rights, and modernity in highland guatemala

MAYA ETHNOLINGUISTIC IDENTITY
violence, cultural rights, and modernity in Highland Guatemala

BRIGITTINE M. FRENCH

The University of Arizona Press
Tucson

The University of Arizona Press
www.uapress.arizona.edu

ISBN-13: 978-0-8165-2767-0 (cloth)
ISBN-13: 978-0-8165-4240-6 (paper)

Cover design by Carrie House, HOUSEdesign llc
Cover images: Mayan Hieroglyphs and Ancient Mayan Sculpture © yummyphotos, shutterstock.com

Library of Congress Cataloging-in-Publication Data
French, Brigittine M.
  Maya ethnolinguistic identity : violence, cultural rights, and modernity in highland Guatemala / Brigittine M. French.
     p. cm.
  Includes bibliographical references and index.
  ISBN 978-0-8165-2767-0 (cloth : alk. paper)
  1. Mayas—Ethnic identity. 2. Mayas—Languages. 3. Mayas—Violence against.
4. Anthropological linguistics—Guatemala. 5. Mayan languages—Guatemala.
6. Language and culture—Guatemala. 7. Politics and culture—Guatemala.
8. Guatemala—Social conditions. 9. Guatemala—Ethnic relations. 10. Guatemala—Politics and government. I. Title.
F1435.3.E72F74 2010
305.80097281—dc22
2009035835

Printed in the United States of America
♾ This paper meets the requirements of ANSI/NISO Z39.48-1992 (Permanence of Paper).

For my mentors,
Nora C. England and Virginia R. Domínguez

Contents

Figures

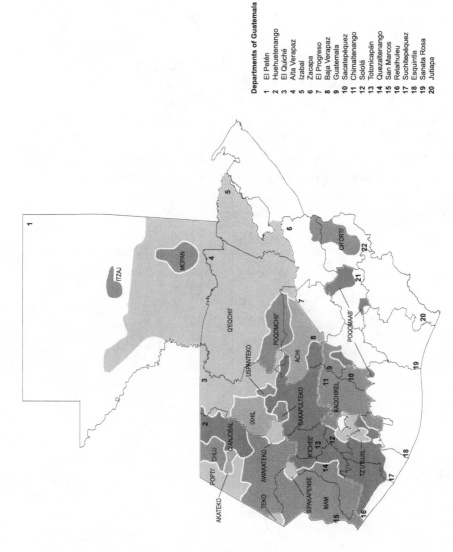

Figure 1. Ethnolinguistic and political map of Guatemala (by Kathryn Dunn).

Preface

As I will examine several strands of scholarly and quotidian ideologies of language in this book, it is important that I make my own ideologies of language visible. After all, this inquiry, like all anthropological projects, is situated in the experiences and preoccupations of its author. I first came to questions about language, politics, and identity through a keen personal sense of the ways in which language becomes implicated in manufacturing social difference. In my own rural, homogeneous, European American community of origin, I was often confronted by the link between social exclusion and linguistic difference. One definitive moment stands out in my memory. When I had just discovered the pleasures of higher education, including the study of "foreign languages" at the collegiate level, a peer from home reprimanded me: "Well, if you want to go to *their* country and speak *their* language, that's fine, but in America we speak English." This was my first self-conscious lesson in understanding the workings of U.S. nationalist linguistic ideology promoting English monolingualism. My peer's criticism was meant to promote social sameness by excluding linguistic Others in service of "Americanness." In retrospect, I came to understand how these ideologies of language and belonging were potent reasons why, while growing up, no one I knew spoke any language other than English, why no one in my family remembered the importance of the Irish and German languages to our immigrant history, and why my home state enthusiastically supported, and eventually passed, English-only legislation. In time, I realized that the doxa of English monolingualism and the social investments in it—despite the presence of multilingual American Indian communities and a history of multilingual European immigration in the Midwest—resonated strongly with the social investments in Spanish monolingualism and its exclusionary politics, which I encountered in Guatemala.

During my first research trip to Guatemala in 1992, I became acquainted with a group of young Maya scholars who were passionately committed to the dual projects of linguistic analysis and social change. Because of the intellectual and interpersonal generosity of our mutual mentor, Dr. Nora C. England, I had the opportunity to become acquainted with linguists of Oxlajuuj Keej Maya' Ajtz'iib' (OKMA). My great admiration for and sustained interaction with OKMA linguists Lolmay, Pakal, Nikte', Waykan, Ajpub', Aj'bee, and B'alam acted as a source of inspiration that brought me back to Guatemala repeatedly during the fifteen years that I intellectually committed myself to the study of linguistic anthropology and social difference. By the time of my first visit in 1992, massive social violence from the civil war in the country had abated, and the projects of Maya ethnonationalist politics were in full swing. Listening to and talking with young Maya linguists involved in what has been variously called the Maya movement, Pan-Mayanism, and Maya ethnonationalism (Fischer and Brown 1996) introduced me to the passions, struggles, and accomplishments they experienced with linguistic revitalization and self-determination, particularly among historically Kaqchikel- and K'iche'-speaking indigenous communities.

I returned to Guatemala in 1994 to investigate empirically the ways in which some Maya people experienced discrimination by Ladinos (non-Indians who account for approximately 45 percent of the national population) in their quotidian lives, and the possible ways that this discrimination and resistance to it were manifested in quotidian discourse. Ethnically mixed public spaces—buses, schools, and markets—were the principal locations of discursive confrontations that Maya scholars and middle-class Ladinos mentioned in a variety of conversations I participated in concerning "ethnic relations" in Guatemala. Guided by these commentaries, I turned to the urban market in Xela (Quetzaltenango)—Guatemala's second-largest city, located within K'iche' ethnolinguistic territory—hoping to witness emergent social changes between ethnically distinct Guatemalans.

My project in Quetzaltenango formed the beginning of a rich and sustained collaboration with Miriam Rodríguez, a bilingual Maya woman born in the early 1970s (like me), a well-educated marketer, and member of a prominent Maya-Kaqchikel family actively involved in Maya cultural revitalization.[1] Together, Miriam and I traversed highland markets listening to, recording, and discussing Maya-Ladino interactions during bargaining transactions in order to detect the negotiation of Maya identity relative to Ladino power in ordinary social discourse. With Miriam's help, my research in the Quetzaltenango markets empirically confirmed what Maya colleagues had been informally saying—that some indigenous people were beginning to challenge the discrimination they faced from Ladinos in quotidian interactions (French 2000). Maya activists ascribed this changing social dynamic in part to Pan-Maya consciousness raising, to which I turned my research.

My experiences with Pan-Maya activism and concomitant scholarly research into language and social inequality intensified. While visiting Miriam and her family in 1996, I was fortunate to witness an historic event in Maya identity politics—El Primer Congreso de Estudios Mayas (the First Congress of Maya Studies). This conference was the first of its kind to be held in Guatemala, a truly remarkable event, given that political discussions about national and "Indian" identity had been historically closed, often secret, and potentially dangerous in the context of recent state-sponsored violence and repression. Even more unprecedented was the constituency of the conference—a mixture of Maya scholars alongside European and North American colleagues, all heatedly engaged in debates about issues concerning Maya identity, Ladino identity, human rights, and Maya linguistic self-determination. Attending the conference left me feeling both excited and ambivalent about my upcoming research project. I greatly admired the work my Maya colleagues were doing and was excited by the prospect of becoming an interlocutor in public dialogues about identity in Guatemala. At the same time, however, my training as an anthropologist left me uneasy with some public positions they took on language and collective identity, especially the isomorphic relationship they asserted between the two. I wondered if some indigenous people might be excluded from such a strongly essentialist position on language and identity, even as I understood that Maya scholars were seeking inclusion for all Maya people in Guatemalan national social and political life.

The politics of shifting inclusions and exclusions were highlighted on December 29, 1996, when the Guatemalan national government signed peace accords with the Unidad Revolucionaria Nacional Guatemalteca (URNG), the leftist umbrella guerrilla organization. This act symbolically ended a brutal, yet publicly unacknowledged, thirty-six-year civil war whose victims were overwhelmingly poor rural Maya citizens (CEH

1999; Sanford 2003). While both parties signed the Accord on the Identity and Rights of Indigenous Peoples, marking the first time in the history of the modern Guatemala nation-state that powerful social institutions had acknowledged the unique rights and identity of indigenous Maya peoples, Mayas were not officially involved in the negotiation process. A significant tension—between equal individual rights within the modern nation and unequal collective representations—was underscored in this act, which ultimately set the stage for further discussions about building a democratic, inclusive, and multicultural Guatemalan nation in the "post-conflict" era.[2]

It was in this post-conflict context—and with the history of several months of fieldwork in Guatemala among bilingual indigenous communities, along with some firsthand knowledge of the Pan-Maya project—that I returned to the highlands between August 1997 and May 1998 to conduct my doctoral research. During that period, I lived and worked in two ethnically mixed urban areas around Antigua and Chimaltenango with indigenous families and neighbors. Both locales are within the ethnolinguistically defined Kaqchikel region and in adjacent state-defined departments. (See fig. 1, which highlights continuities and disjunctures between national political-administrative departments with linguistically defined Maya groups in the country.) While residing in these urban environs and visiting their predominantly "Indian" *municipios*, I also began studying the Kaqchikel language that had swirled around me in the markets and in Miriam's home. I formally started learning Kaqchikel with a bilingual speaker from neighboring Lake Atitlán and continued studying with a woman from Santa María de Jesús for the duration of my fieldwork.

In my return visits to Guatemala in 1999 and 2001, I was received as a fledgling scholar. Generously, and perhaps skeptically, Lolmay and Waykan of OKMA invited me to present a paper on their panel in the Cuarto Congreso de Mayistas (Fourth Congress of Mayanists). Their invitation was both thrilling and daunting, as it underscored the responsibility that I, as a foreign researcher, had in presenting my findings to indigenous audiences in Guatemala (England 1998; Warren 1998). The persistent unfolding of an omnipresent tension between strategic essentialism, which Mayas use as part of their political project, and a constructivist perspective, which some North American anthropologists (myself included) use to combat naturalized cultural difference (Fischer 1996; Reynolds 1997; Warren 1998), figures centrally in my orientation toward linguistic ideologies and the arguments presented in this book. My efforts to work out this tension and give it a theoretically productive turn are themselves tied to the academic identity of a U.S. anthropologist whose intellectual maturity developed in the milieu of Pan-Maya cultural activism. Consequently, the theoretical issues I address in this book cannot be separated from my recognition that Maya linguists have indelibly shaped the direction of my research. It is to them that I owe the greatest debt.

Acknowledgments

Ideas, like the language we use to give them shape, are products of multiple, overlapping, and conflicting discursive exchanges. Throughout the process of researching and writing this book, I have been fortunate to have several remarkable interlocutors. The linguists of Oxlajuuj Keej Maya' Ajtz'iib' (OKMA), Lolmay, Nikte', Ajpub', Waykan, B'alam, and Aj'bee, have my deepest gratitude and respect. Without their challenges, help, skepticism, and generosity, there would have been no project. *Matyox k'a ri'*. Nora England continually supported this work with pragmatic questions, no-nonsense critiques, and a great deal of camaraderie during the moments when I needed them most. Virginia R. Domínguez carefully and passionately taught me what intellectual integrity and academic excellence are all about through numerous hours of mentoring. It is my great hope that she will see some small measure of her influence in the pages that follow.

Takis Poulakos selflessly read more versions of this book than I can count. I am indebted to Laurie Graham, Mike Chibnik, and Mercedes Niño-Murcia for reading earlier drafts of this book and providing thoughtful suggestions that made the manuscript stronger. Jennifer Reynolds has been and continues to be the best *compañera* a linguistic anthropologist could hope for. I thank Allyson Carter at the University of Arizona Press, who encouraged this project in its earliest professional stages and continued to support it throughout the production process. The anonymous reviewers for the University of Arizona Press extended considerable time and attention to my ideas and their presentation in the manuscript. These reviewers' clear generosity and formidable challenges made the final product analytically and ethnographically sharper. I appreciate Gustavo Arambula's careful attention to my transcriptions and translations in this text and his constant good humor as we worked on them together. I sincerely thank Sondi Burnell, Veronica Clark, and Alexis Stern for their diligent work with manuscript and bibliography preparation. I thank Katie

Dunn for creating the maps included in the text and Whitney Knopf for conceptualizing a fine index for the book.

Time to research and write is also the product of significant exchanges at institutional and interpersonal levels. I gratefully acknowledge financial support from the T. Anne Cleary Fellowship for International Research from the University of Iowa, The Ballard Fellowship in the Social Sciences and Humanities from the University of Iowa, the Andrew W. Mellon Foundation Postdoctoral Fellowship Program, and the Committee for Support of Faculty Scholarship at Grinnell College. Three amazing women, Sarah French, Lily French, and Ann French, gave me precious time to write whenever I asked. Nick Drahozal and Nysio Poulakos offered me enduring patience and bright smiles during my many hours at the computer.

I gratefully acknowledge the kind permission of the following publishers to reproduce earlier versions of my work. Chapter 1 appeared as "Maya Ethnolinguistic Identity: Violence and Cultural Rights in Bilingual Kaqchikel Communities" in *Bilingualism and Identity: Spanish at the Crossroads with Other Languages*, edited by Mercedes Niño-Murcia and Jason Rothman, 2008, 127–150 (John Benjamins Publishing Company, Amsterdam/Philadelphia, www.benjamins.com). An earlier version of chapter 2 appeared as "The Politics of Mayan Linguistics in Guatemala: Native Speakers, Expert Analysts, and the Nation" in *Pragmatics* 13(3–4): 483–498 (International Pragmatics Association).

Abbreviations

ALMG	Academia de Lenguas Mayas de Guatemala (Mayan Languages Academy of Guatemala)
ALMK	Academia de Lengua Maya K'iche' (K'iche' Mayan Language Academy)
CEH	Comisión para el Esclarecimiento Histórico (Commission for Historical Clarification)
CIRMA	Centro de Investigaciones Regionales de Mesoamérica (Center for Regional Investigations of Mesoamerica)
COMG	Consejo de Organizaciones Mayas de Guatemala (Council of Mayan Organizations of Guatemala)
DIJEBI	Dirección General de Educación Bilingüe Intercultural (General Directorate of Bilingual and Intercultural Education)
IIN	Instituto Indigenista Nacional (National Indigneous Institute)
NGO	Nongovernmental organization
OKMA	Oxlajuuj Keej Maya' Ajtz'iib'
PLFM	Proyecto Lingüístico Francisco Marroquín
SIL	Summer Institute of Linguistics
UNICEF	United Nations Children's Fund
URL	Universidad Rafael Landívar (Rafael Landívar University)
URNG	Unidad Revolucionaria Nacional Guatemalteca (National Guatemalan Revolutionary Unity)
USAC	Universidad de San Carlos (San Carlos National University)

MAYA ETHNOLINGUISTIC IDENTITY

violence, cultural rights, and modernity in Highland Guatemala

Introduction

Language Ideologies, Collective Identities, and the Politics of Exclusion

ON MAY 5, 2003, in an historically unprecedented move, the Guatemalan Congress passed the Ley de Idiomas Nacionales, or National Languages Law. The law formally recognized that "the right of the peoples and indigenous communities to their cultural identity in accordance with their values, their language, and their customs, should be fundamentally guaranteed by the State" (Congreso de la República de Guatemala 2003). Such an explicit invocation of guaranteed "rights" relative to indigenous "cultural identity" and "language" was a markedly new position for the Guatemalan state. Only a few years earlier, in 1999, a national referendum to co-officialize all twenty-one Mayan languages spoken in Guatemala alongside Spanish was defeated.[1] Indeed, the majority of twentieth-century state-directed professional involvement with Mayan languages in Guatemala was explicitly aimed at ameliorating the "problem" of Maya cultural difference manifested through and emblematic in Mayan linguistic difference. In this way, the idealized erasure of Mayan languages through the promise of Spanish linguistic assimilation among indigenous communities functioned in service of homogeneous nation building (French 2003). In short, during much of the twentieth century, national visions for creating a unified Guatemala were predicated upon and committed to transforming Mayan-speaking *indios* into Spanish-speaking *guatemaltecos*.

Perhaps even more impressive than this marked shift from a long-standing practice of assimilation to an official state policy guaranteeing the rights of indigenous languages and identity was the constituency of its supporters. Not surprisingly, Maya scholars and activists rallied behind the policy and became its staunch advocates. This was quite expected, given that their work at various levels during the latter half of the twentieth century for the promotion of linguistic rights included such efforts as the development of a unified orthography for Mayan languages, the creation of the Guatemalan Mayan Languages Academy, the implementation of standardization projects, and grassroots literacy efforts in several highland communities. These self-conscious efforts, directed toward both recognizing and promoting Mayan languages, have been understood as integral components of democratic multicultural reform within the nation (Brown 1998; French 1999; England 2003), reform that this new law was promising to realize.

More surprising, however, was the fact that the new law was codified by the president of the Congress, Jose Efrain Ríos Montt. Ríos Montt was none other than the former general/president of Guatemala, who had been complicit with acts of genocide against the Maya population during La Violencia (1978–1984) just decades earlier, when more than two hundred thousand people were killed by Guatemalan military forces (Carmack 1988; CEH 1999; Sanford 2003). Paradoxically, Ríos Montt officially endorsed the cultural rights of the very people his government had sought to violently purge from the body politic of the nation through acts of horrific genocide that have yet to be brought to justice in the "post-conflict" era (Sanford 2008).

The ironies entailed in the Ley de Idiomas Nacionales situate the consideration of language and identity in Guatemala among urban highland Maya communities squarely between, on the one hand, the contemporary cultural rights claims of Maya scholars/activists, and, on the other hand, the recent history of extreme violence against them by the state. These issues are at the heart of a nation which, since the beginning of the nation-building period during the early nineteenth century, has been erected upon the stark opposition between two groups: "Indians" and Ladinos (Smith 1990b). Despite the diversity of racial identification and classification in the early post-colonial history of Guatemala (T. Little-Siebold 2001; C. Little Siebold 2001), the nationalist project has been structured around the Guatemalan/indigenous binary.[2] In this context, "Ladino" refers to the minority of Guatemala's twelve million citizens who are of mixed European—usually Spanish—and indigenous ancestry. "Indian" refers to the majority of Guatemala's population who are members of the twenty-one academically defined Maya ethnolinguistic groups: Achi, Akateko, Awakateko, Ch'orti, Chuj, Itzaj, Ixil, Kaqchikel, K'iche',

Mam, Mopan, Popti', Poqomchi', Poqomam, Q'anjob'al, Q'eqchi', Sakapulteko, Sipakapense, Teko, Tz'utujiil, and Uspanteko. These ethnolinguistic groups belong to a larger group of approximately thirty Mayan
languages spoken by numerous communities in other Mesoamerican
countries, including Mexico, Belize, and Honduras, that descended from
a common ancestral language spoken around four thousand years ago in
the lowlands (England 2003:733).[3]

Seizing upon the conceptual opposition between the two social categories of Indian and Ladino, the Guatemalan state has actively circulated
a racialized conception of "Indians" as an undifferentiated, inherently
inferior group that has stood stubbornly in the way of national progress, unity, and development. Modeling its nationhood after Western
paradigms of nation building that presuppose the necessity of cultural
homogeneity for collective unification at the national level (Gellner 1983;
Handler 1988), the state circulated discourses according to which being
Guatemalan has meant to be Ladino, and being Ladino has meant to be
non-Indian, leaving little room for indigenous identity within the Guatemalan nation-state. Within this commonplace and hegemonic logic, the
persistence of the "Indian problem" became the bane of the nationalist
project to craft a homogenous national community. As an integral part of
that process, the modern Guatemalan state has sought to eradicate cultural differences in order to create a unified nation through a variety of
social, economic, and political means, including (but certainly not limited to) those efforts specifically directed at the linguistic assimilation of
Maya-speaking populations to Spanish through scholarly linguistic analysis, religious conversion, bilingual education, compulsory Spanish literacy classes, and military service.

Enduring essential constructs of "Indians" as inherently backward, un-
civilized, and ignorant have supported a structurally racist society in which
indigenous people have been marginalized in land tenure systems, educational opportunities, and formal political involvement due to their "natural" inferiority during much of the twentieth century (Casaus Arzú 1992;
Hale 2006). These powerful notions of immutable "Indian" difference
grounded in racialized notions of identity have had profound material and
violent consequences for the majority Maya population. In fact, exclusive
constructions of national identity that structurally marginalize part of the
population often foster the conditions for state-sponsored violence against

Others within the nation's borders (Hayden 1996; DeVotta 2004). Hayden argues that essentialist constructions of collective identity in the context of homogeneous nation building can be "a matter of making heterogeneous communities unimaginable. In formal terms, the point has been to implement an essentialist definition of the nation . . . the brutal negation of social reality in order to reconstruct it. It is this reconstruction that turns the imagination of a community into a process that produces real victims" (1996:784). Hayden's point applies to nation-building strategies in Guatemala all too well: essentialist constructions of Indian identity grounded in racialized notions of immutable difference were situated as antithetical to definitions of Guatemalan national identity. These constructions, in turn, played a productive role in generating the social and political factors that paved the way for state-sponsored violence against Maya populations that resulted in the most extreme manifestation of racism—genocide (Menchú 1983; Montejo 1987; Carmack 1988; Grandin 2004). From the late 1970s to the mid-1980s, the military, under the leadership of presidents/generals Lucas García and Ríos Montt, unleashed a brutal campaign against Maya populations. During the worst years of the violence, at least two hundred thousand people were killed and another 1.5 million people were displaced, the overwhelming majority of whom were indigenous Maya people (Montejo 1987; Carmack 1988; Wilson 1995; CEH 1999; Sanford 2003). The United Nations–sponsored truth commission's investigation found that the state committed genocide against the Maya population, meaning "acts committed with intent to destroy, in whole or in part, a national, ethnic, racial or religious group" as defined by the 1948 United Nations Genocide Convention (CEH 1999). The horrors of state-sponsored violence in Guatemala were brought to international attention by Maya-K'iche' activist Rigoberta Menchú through her testimony, *I, Rigoberta Menchú: An Indian Woman in Guatemala* (1983). Menchú's work in exile as an activist for indigenous rights earned her the Nobel Peace Prize in 1992 and helped to garner international pressure for the United Nations–brokered peace accord eventually signed in the final month of 1996.

In the context of indigenous activism with focused political, intellectual, and financial support from the international community (particularly the United States, Europe, and Japan), some Maya people became committed to a vibrant ethnonationalist movement in the post-Violence era.[4] Participants in what has been variously called El Moviemento Maya (the Maya movement), Maya ethnonationalism, and Pan-Mayanism seek to promote Maya cultural difference within the nation-state and to craft a collective Maya identity in the face of a national policy of assimilation and violence (COMG 1991; Cojtí Cuxil 1991, 1994, 1995; Fischer and Brown 1996; Warren 1998). This is a movement launched both against the nation-state and in favor of the nation as reconstituted and redefined by the politics of cultural difference. The Maya movement's cultural revitalization project, based centrally (although not exclusively) around the Mayan languages, is linked to the dual political objectives of promoting cultural autonomy for Maya peoples and of reconfiguring the Guatemalan nation into a multilingual and multicultural democracy.

Central to the pursuit of the Maya movement's ongoing goals of cultural self-determination and progressive political reform within the Guatemalan state is the strategically essential linking of Mayan languages with the ideal of a unified Maya *pueblo* (people/nation) (French 1999). Among various aspects of culture that become objectified to form the foundation upon which a collective identity may be erected, language holds a unique place. Considered to be the most fundamental essence of Maya identity, Mayan languages function as "the presumably shared content of group identity that distinguishes the group from other collective groups with rights in the nation" (Handler 1988:15). This nationalist language ideology linking Mayan languages with the ideal of collective Maya identity has acted as an effective means for structuring notions of difference and legitimizing calls for cultural autonomy within the Guatemalan nation-state. Indeed, the few but important victories Maya leaders have won involve the state's recognition of difference based upon the cultural distinctiveness of Mayan languages and their provisional inclusion in the Guatemalan national community.

Ethnolinguistic Identity Projects

These two radically different projects—the Pan-Maya project to valorize cultural difference and the Guatemalan national project to obliterate it— share three common features that have profoundly affected collective understandings of language and identity in contemporary Guatemala. First, both projects rely on an essentialized construction of language and indigenous identity, which means that both take the *cultural* system of ideas about social and linguistic relationships to be an *inherent* one (Irvine 1989; emphasis mine). Second, the Guatemalan state and its embodied forces are key mediators of both essentialist projects to erase or valorize Maya cultural difference in the recent twentieth-century history of the country. Finally, as political projects that mobilize a nationalist ideology of language for very different ends, both produce ideologies that have been lived and experienced by local Maya communities in myriad, heterogeneous ways.

Despite the homogenizing efforts of both projects, a diversity of language ideologies circulates among Maya communities in the Guatemalan highlands. In fact, throughout most post-conquest history, indigenous peoples in Guatemala have most frequently understood themselves in terms of diverse local identities, not as a unified translocal indigenous group. The *municipio* (roughly, county) has been the locus of indigenous identity, an identity that is distinct not only from that of Ladinos but also from that of Maya people from other communities within the academically defined ethnolinguistic group (Tax 1937; Brintnall 1979; Bunzel 1959; Warren 1978; Watanabe 1992; Reynolds 2002).[5] Thus, on the ground, indigenous Maya identity has often been defined by participation in local communities' histories, discourses, and social networks, rather than by membership in a particular ethnolinguistic community.

All of this means that configuring the relationship between Mayan languages and collective identity in contemporary Guatemala has resulted in a series of ongoing, competing *projects*. That is to say, constructions of language and collective identity are strategic efforts undertaken by several institutions (the government, the military, the educational system, the church) and social actors (linguists, scholars, activists, and speakers); they are political, moral, and affective investments; and they have ongoing consequences for individuals and institutions in the unfolding of local, national, and international arenas. In the pages that follow, I take up an investigation of some of these strategic efforts, situated understandings, and effects of competing ethnolinguistic identity projects. I do so primarily by examining written and spoken metalinguistic discourses that are propagated by powerful agents (the government; the military; and academic, activist, and missionary linguists) and their interlocutors in some bilingual highland Kaqchikel and K'iche' communities.

Kaqchikel and K'iche' ethnolinguistic communities are unique in many ways. They are among the demographically largest Maya ethnolinguistic groups in Guatemala; Kaqchikel has around 405,000 speakers and K'iche' has approximately one million. Historically, many of the Maya movement's most visible leaders have come from Kaqchikel and K'iche' communities. It is also important to note that there are very high levels of Spanish bilingualism among K'iche' and Kaqchikel groups that further problematize the possibility of an essential ethnolinguistic identification among these communities. Conservative estimates are that 86.9 percent of Kaqchikels and 95 percent of K'iche' speakers are bilingual (Richards and Richards 1990). Furthermore, sociolinguistic research has shown that this phenomenon indicates a transitory bilingualism leading to a long-term shift to Spanish monolingualism, particularly among young indigenous people in urban areas (Brown 1991; Garzon 1991; England 1998). It is equally important to note that these Kaqchikel and K'iche' communities have been more subjected than other communities to the economic, cultural, and political forces of national society due to their proximity to Ladino power centers (Maxwell 1996) and, in some cases, the militarization of their communities (CEH 1999).[6] Therefore, the histories and experiences of urban Kaqchikel and K'iche' communities shaping ideologies of language and identity are markedly different from those of Mayas living in other parts of the country and in other Mesoamerican nation-states. This means that the analysis I present here is intended to offer a necessarily partial understanding of the ways in which state violence and cultural revitalization have been propagated institutionally as well as experienced locally by some urban highland Maya communities with high levels of bilingualism among demographically larger Mayan languages. I hope this work may provide a comparative model for the study of language ideologies, violence, cultural rights, and identity among demographically smaller Maya ethnolinguistic groups and Maya communities with different historical and political relations with the nation-states in which they reside.

To be clear, the various metalinguistic discourses I analyze in this book are not from particular communities that are bound in the typical ethnographic sense. Rather, I look at metalinguistic talk about Mayan languages produced in shifting but persistent academic, geographic, and demographic groups, particularly in Kaqchikel and K'iche' areas of the country. Following Handler's approach to the analysis of ethnonationalism and cultural politics (1988:26), I want to underscore that the narratives, metalinguistic discourse, incidents, and conversations that I analyze in the following pages are unified only by my own analytic and interpretative perspective. I make these choices explicit in an effort to limit ethnographic typification (Abu-Lughod 1992). Though limited to specific institutions and social actors that are prominent in a few highland Maya communities, this investigation will enable me to show how some individuals in urban, bilingual, indigenous communities do indeed disrupt the essentializing projects upon which both the repressive and the democratizing projects have been built. I also aim to show that, in particular, urban Kaqchikel citizens of the Chimaltenango department, as well as their K'iche' contemporaries in places like Rabinal and Momostenango, articulate alternative notions about language and identity in terms that are not isomorphic with essentialized ethnolinguistic identification. Instead, some Maya social actors are more concerned with relationships between language and modernity in heterogeneous ways.

Ideologies of Language, Exclusion, and Modernity

I undertake this inquiry into metalinguistic discourse, language, and Maya identity from the developing theoretical perspective offered by recent linguistic anthropological scholarship on ideologies of language—that is to say, from the situated analysis of language within the explicit context of broader political and ideological developments in society (Schieffelin, Woolard, and Kroskrity 1998; Blommaert 1999; Kroskrity 2000). A focus on ideologies of language enables me to explicitly link linguistic forms and functions with consciousness and social positions, as well as the making of hegemonic power relations. To be sure, there is a related history of sociolinguistic and anthropological inquiries into "language conflict" and "language politics" in multilingual communities where there have been self-conscious struggles over etholinguistic identity. Irvine explains:

> To proponents of putative ethnolinguistic unities, it has seemed "natural" to suppose that language itself creates community; that an aggregate of people who could be said to "share" a language must, ipso facto, share

other things and jointly participate in a social formation of some specifiable kind. It has been the hallmark of linguistic anthropology, however, to problematize these relationships and their constituent terms. (1996:123)

Like other new inquiries based upon ideologies of language, my research draws upon the established line of anthropological linguistic research that has thoroughly debated and debunked the validity of an essentialized understanding of language and collective identity (Boas [1911] 1966; Hymes 1984; Irvine 1996). As Woolard (1998) underscores, however, this body of research has yet to analyze "*how* the view of languages as discrete, distinctive entities and as emblematic of self and community come to take hold in so many different settings" (18; emphasis mine). The inquiry undertaken in this book into language ideologies and collective identities in Guatemala responds to Woolard's call for new analysis that will show the processes by which essentialized ideologies of language become efficacious in particular contexts, such as in the powerful linking of Mayan languages with a collective indigenous identity mobilized in Guatemala by competing political projects.

At the ethnographic level, my analysis here highlights some of the pragmatic meanings of Kaqchikel and K'iche' as they emerge in various local contexts. In this way, my work draws upon the perspectives of "ethnography of communication" (Hymes 1962; Bricker 1973; Gossen 1974; Haviland 1977) and "language maintenance and shift" (Brown 1998; Garzon 1998b; Richards 1998) in the study of Mayan languages and their speakers, and advances these orientations with a keen eye toward identifying the political work entailed in making meaning (Schieffelin, Woolard, and Kroskrity 1998; Blommaert 1999; Kroskrity 2000), as well as toward discerning the ideological work entailed in linking meanings of language with social systems of inclusion and exclusion.

The recent work of Bauman and Briggs, *Voices of Modernity: Language Ideologies and the Politics of Inequality* (2003), offers a productive theoretical framework in this endeavor to track the relationships between language ideologies and collective identity as they structure social inclusions and exclusions in post-conflict Guatemala. Bauman and Briggs highlight the ways in which ideologies of language are central to creating and naturalizing exclusions of particular social groups based upon the "moral and political loading of language forms" with collective identities (Irvine 1989). In particular, Bauman and Briggs direct analytic attention to construction of modernity and tradition as one of the most important ways through which language forms and collective identities become linked.

Bauman and Briggs regard the construction of modernity and tradition as central to the social reproduction of inequality, such as the kind of structural inequality that often characterizes post-colonial multiethnic nations like Guatemala. Following other scholars of modernity, Bauman and Briggs illustrate the promulgation of epistemological and ideological orientations of constructing modernity among European (and European American) intellectual thought from the seventeenth to the early twentieth century in order to show how modernist assumptions and projects became seemingly universal, historically transcendent, and hegemonic (3–4). Most importantly, their work on modernity explains how constitutive aspects of modern society—the rise of capitalism, the centrality of the nation-state, the development of new class, race, and gender-based distinctions, and the privileging of ideas of progress and science (Hinton 2002:7)—became naturalized and exported to the rest of the world in service of domination during colonial and post-colonial eras.

Going beyond other scholars' analyses of modernity, Bauman and Briggs shed light on the overlooked but important role that constructions of language and tradition played in the precarious project of creating and naturalizing modernity in ways that justify social exclusions (2003:17). They show how ideologies of language became central mechanisms for structuring difference in such a way that modernity necessarily excluded such social categories as the female, the rural, the working class, the unsophisticated, the oral, and the Oriental, precisely because of their indexical links to "tradition" as a mediating force in the alignment of premodernity to modernity (2003:11). While Bauman and Briggs's specific inquiry into language ideologies and uses of tradition is grounded in an historical analysis of the ways that European ideas about language and modernity became deproventialized and used in dominating the rest of the world (2003:3), their theoretical project resonates with the very contemporary struggle among Maya communities in Guatemala to define Mayan languages in empowering terms and to create collective identities within an explicitly hierarchical and modernist framework. As I will show in the chapters that follow, close attention to aspects of "modern" society

—especially to the centrality of the nation-state as it propagated violence against its indigenous citizens, to the development of class-, race-, and gender-based distinctions as they relate to systems of exclusion, and to the privileging of scientific linguistics to regiment Mayan languages—is essential to understanding ideologies of Mayan languages among bilingual urbanized Kaqchikel and K'iche' communities in Guatemala. These factors indelibly influence the competing political projects and their complications outlined in this book.

Let me provide two brief examples that delineate the centrality of modernity and tradition in discourses about Mayan languages in postconflict Guatemala that will be taken up in greater detail in the chapters that follow. In one of his many treatises on linguistic revitalization and democratic multiculturalism in Guatemala, Dr. Demetrio Cojtí, linguist and foremost visible leader of the Maya ethnonationalist movement, explained the importance of tradition and modernity to the political project of Pan-Maya cultural revitalization and indigenous unification in the following way: "The Mayanist movement is at once predominantly conservative on the cultural plane and predominantly innovative and revolutionary on the political and economic plane. For that reason, it is said that the Maya movement's path leads not only to Tikal (traditionalism) but also to New York and Tokyo (modernism)" (1997:78).[7]

While Cojtí explicitly underscores the centrality of both the "traditional" and the "modern" to his project of Pan-Maya linguistic revitalization and political unification, similar, yet not identical concerns with modernity and tradition circulate in quotidian discourse throughout many bilingual highland Maya villages in the country. I encountered one of these concerns during the spring of 1999, chatting over coffee with Ixmucane, who had just begun studying linguistics at the postgraduate level. She talked of her newfound commitments to Pan-Maya principles, in particular, her determination to speak more frequently in her native language, Q'anjob'al. The problem, at least as she described it to me, was that people from her local community often challenged her turn toward "tradition." Ixmucane recalled the sharp words of a classmate who encountered her listening to American hip-hop music on her CD player. He teased, "¿Vos sos muy maya ahora, porque no escuches la marimba en vivo y saludarme en dilecto?" ("You're so Maya now, why don't you listen to live marimba music and greet me in our language?")

These two examples of elite and vernacular discourses highlight the importance of notions of modernity and tradition as they are implicitly or explicitly mapped onto language and Maya identities in post-conflict Guatemala. Marked in the discourse of Demetrio Cojtí and his compatriots, such notions confirm the explanatory power that Bauman and Briggs's theoretical account has for contemporary inquiries about language ideologies, collective identities, and social inequality:

> Constructing language and tradition and placing them in relationship to science and politics continues to play a key role in producing and naturalizing new modernist projects, new sets of legislators, and new forms of social inequality. . . . Indeed it would be difficult to imagine a time that the power of this process was more apparent than the end of the twentieth century and the beginning of the twenty-first. (2003:301)

The active construction of "tradition" and "modernity" through both science and politics in Guatemala are central to the creation of exclusive definitions of identity among bilingual highland Kaqchikel and K'iche' communities that privilege ethnolinguistic identifications at the expense of other axes of sameness.

Taking up Bauman and Briggs's project of tracing the productive role language ideologies play in producing social inequality within modernist projects, this book aims to show the ways in which some ideologies of Mayan languages and their linking with tradition are implicated in the crafting of collective identities and the concomitant social exclusions that such craftings perpetuate. Part of the inquiry I conduct into ideologies of Mayan languages, tradition, and social inequality (chapters 1, 2, and 4) supports Bauman and Briggs's historical analysis in the post-conflict Guatemalan context to show that notions of tradition, when mapped onto language, function to further hegemonic power relations that serve to subordinate indigenous Guatemalans. Another part of the inquiry goes beyond Bauman and Briggs to show that tradition, as it is used to structure language ideologies, does not work solely in service of maintaining hegemonic systems. Rather, I argue, *tradition does not occupy a fixed position in the structuring of social relations that form gestures of exclusion and constructions of Otherness.* I recall Gal's flexible notion of hegemony, namely, that hegemonic systems are necessarily "partial, productive of contradictory consciousnesses, fragile, unstable, and vulnerable to the making of counter-hegemonies" (1998:321), and bring it to bear on Bauman and Briggs's critical project in order to complicate their analysis (in chapters 3, 4, 5, and 6). More specifically, my ethnographic examination of some of the Mayan language ideologies at play in contemporary highland Kaqchikel and K'iche' communities allows me to show that tradition and its ideological links with language can, in fact, be used to challenge the unintended homogenizing effects and unanticipated tacit exclusions that democratic social projects like the Maya movement create.

Methods and Mapping Language and Identity

Within this highly charged context, there is, necessarily, a diverse set of language ideologies linked with collective experiences and identities, each link embedded differently within the modernist framework that permeates the Guatemalan social, political, and economic landscape. I investigate some links primarily through analyses of metalinguistic discourse and the scholarly regimentation of language (descriptive and prescriptive linguistics). Metalinguistic discourse and the scholarly regimentation of language are two key areas in which ideology impacts language—the former is explicit talk about language and the latter is the ordering and structuring of language by expert social actors (Woolard 1998). Certainly, ideology is created through linguistic practice, although that inquiry remains outside the scope of this project.[8]

To investigate the ideological articulation of language with collective identity in Guatemala through the scholarly/activist regimentation of language and through metalinguistic discourse, I collected a disparate assortment of data. During various fieldwork trips to highland Kaqchikel and K'iche' communities from 1995 through 2001, I engaged in participant observation, open-ended interviews, casual conversations, scholarly debates, library research, and sociolinguistic interviews. Working with the variety of data and contexts I analyze in the pages that follow, I further contextualize the specific data and their collection in each relevant section. From the outset, though, I want to underscore that I had the great fortune to work closely with Miriam Rodríguez from January until May of 1998. As I mentioned in the preface, Miriam was my research assistant and collected a great deal of the sociolinguistic interview data I analyze in chapters 4 and 5.[9]

In the pages that follow, I use a variety of metalinguistic data to create a partial map of some ideological configurations of language and identity among bilingual urban geographical, intellectual, and demographic Maya communities. To be clear about the presentation of metalinguistic discourse, let me briefly explain the transcription conventions and analytic choices I have made in representing recorded spoken and written discourse. As Ochs points out, transcription is a selective process that reflects the author's theoretical and analytic goals (1979:44). In the transcripts that follow throughout this book, I am particularly concerned with the indexical linking of Mayan languages and Spanish with collective experiences and identifications that include recurring themes of violence, collective identity, and modernity in various spatial/temporal contexts. For this reason, I have used a standard Spanish orthography to convey as clearly as possible the expression of ideas that link language with identity in metalinguistic discourse. Generally, I have followed O'Connell and Kowal's prescription, based upon their analysis of transcription methodology, that analysts make only those notations in transcription that keep with the purposes of the research question (2000:247). Consequently, I have tried to represent morphological as well as syntactic features of nonstandard Maya Spanish that include variation in subject/verb agreement, tense, and grammatical gender because these are marked forms of Maya bilingualism that native speakers have a keen metalinguistic awareness of in speech. Furthermore, I have represented pauses, false starts, and other aspects of conversational speech. Finally, I have taken care to accurately represent discourse structures in Spanish that often mark "Maya ways of telling," including parallel structure and repetition (Brody 1986). These discursive features are important because they pragmatically underscore authority and affect in speakers' lived understandings of indexical connections between language and identity. I have not represented phonetic and phonological variations, since they are outside the direct scope of my analysis. A list of transcription conventions appears in the appendix.

The first chapter, "The Paradox of Ethnolinguistic Identity: Essentialisms, State-Sponsored Violence, and Cultural Rights," situates the project of Maya ethnolinguistic identity theoretically at the center of anthropological debates about essentialism, as well as ethnographically between a history of violence and contemporary cultural rights claims. The chapter demonstrates that both the Guatemalan state and the Pan-Maya movement have linked Mayan languages to indigenous identity in immutable ways. It argues that such essentializing ideologies of language from both sides have been productive in structuring radically different political projects. This argument is borne out through a discursive analysis of survivor narratives of linguistic assimilation in the years leading up to and during La Violencia among highland Kaqchikel (and other) communities. This analysis is juxtaposed with a consideration of a recent linguistics project centered on the creation of Kaqchikel neologisms.

In chapter 2, "Political Linguistics: Expert Linguists and Modernist Epistemologies in the Guatemalan Nation," I attend to institutions of power (the state, the Department of Education, and nongovernmental organizations) and to expert linguists involved in them who promote particular ethnonationalist ideologies of language and concomitant forms of collective identities. This chapter shows how, in their counterhegemonic efforts, Maya scholar-activists appropriate and, indeed, privilege linguistic science—an explicitly modernist epistemology—as a valuable tool for challenging national social inequality. The chapter traces this appropriation of science as it emerged in a recent history of the transformation of linguistics as an authoritative regime of knowledge linked to various political projects. It begins with an analysis of the grammars of Kaqchikel produced in the 1930s by missionary linguists who claimed scientific authority on the basis of their project to assimilate Maya people into the state and the Christian faith in order to produce a homogeneous Guatemalan people. It proceeds with an analysis of the substantially different Mayan language grammars produced in the 1970s by Maya linguists in collaboration with secular North American linguists, whose claims to authority rested on the right of Maya people to represent their own languages for the sake of both "good science" and the recognition of cultural rights manifested through linguistic recognition. The chapter argues that scientific epistemology—what Bauman and Briggs (2003) identify as the hegemonic "wellspring of modernity" (4)—is used to resist the national hegemony that excludes Mayas. Maya linguists use linguistic science to challenge the explicitly homogenizing and exclusionary goals of what Anderson (1991) calls the "most universally legitimate political form" of modern times.

While Maya scholars have used linguistic science for counterhegemonic purposes to challenge their exclusion from the Guatemalan nation, their efforts also confirm what Bauman and Briggs suggest—namely, that "contemporary critical projects themselves bolster key foundations of the modernity that they claim to challenge" (2003:309). Indeed, as the Maya movement creates new experts to regiment language through linguistic science, it tends to tacitly exclude Maya groups that do not clearly fit within or subscribe to ethnolinguistic definitions of indigenous identity. In this way, Pan-Maya scholarly activism tends to contribute to the creation of what Bauman and Briggs call the "power/knowledge syndrome," in which the intellectual is authorized, on the basis of claims to superior knowledge, to legislate the "maintenance and perfection of the social order" (2003:309). In this case, the social order that progressive Maya legislators seek to perfect is the essential connection between Mayan languages and a collective Maya identity supported by their scientific analyses that, in turn, marginalizes other definitions of Maya identity based upon alternative epistemologies.

In the trajectory Bauman and Briggs (2003) enumerate, the construction of "tradition" and its ideological mapping onto language is a necessary condition to further instantiating hegemony and social inequality based upon the exclusions of Others that it justifies. However, as an examination of some locally held ideologies of language in bilingual Kaqchikel and K'iche' communities that I discuss in chapters 3, 4, and 5 allows me to demonstrate, the invocation of tradition—both assumptions about it and claims to it—can be used to challenge nascent hegemonies and burgeoning expert legislators. In the Guatemalan case, Maya linguists' project of linguistic unification and concomitant Pan-Maya identification is challenged by locally held and experienced ideologies of linguistic tradition. In other words, local constructions of language and tradition challenge the tacit gestures of exclusion that the critical Pan-Maya project unwittingly re-inscribes, even as its leaders fight for indigenous inclusion at the national level.

In order to demonstrate this argument, I examine ideologies of language in the Achi linguistic community, ideologies of language in the metalinguistic discourse of urban wage-earning Mayas from Chimaltenango, and the gendered ideologies of language implicated in the sociolinguistic and ethnographic construction of the "traditional" monolingual Maya woman. Chapter 3, "Traditional Histories, Local Selves, and Challenges to Linguistic Unification," inquires into the ways in which local communities sometimes challenge Maya scholars' expert scientific knowledge based upon locally held ideologies of language grounded in the historical tradition of the community. This chapter situates Pan-Maya conceptions of Mayan languages as the essential component of collective indigenous identity against local struggles to define locally spoken varieties as distinct from others. Specifically, it discusses local debates about linguistic difference and sameness through an analysis of the K'iche'-Achi debate to show how debates about language borders are implicated in competing versions of historical tradition and collective identity.

Chapter 4, "Modernity and Local Linguistic Ideologies in Chimaltenango," examines the grassroots language ideologies among a group of bilingual urban Maya-Kaqchikels from the Chimaltenago department, an area undergoing an increasingly rapid language shift to Spanish and often categorized as a "lost" community by Maya scholars/activists. The analysis shows that Maya citizens of Chimaltenango identify themselves as actors in a "modern" present within which life is perceived to be materially, economically, and socially better than it had been in the past. Within this narrative of "progress," their language ideologies link Kaqchikel with undesirable, old ways of living, and Spanish with modern, desirable ways of life. Nevertheless, an emergent, explicit discourse about the value of culture reconfigures the tradition of Kaqchikel as a valuable, objectified piece of culture for "modern" identity due to Pan-Maya linguistic activism. It makes the case that such ideologies, paradoxically, encourage linguistic assimilation to Spanish and expedite language shift, even as they increase the symbolic capital of Kaqchikel and other Mayan languages in the area.

Chapter 5, "Traditional Maya Women and Linguistic Reproduction," offers a reconsideration of sociolinguistic data from several Kaqchikel communities (San Martín, Comalapa, Tecpán) along with my own data from Chimaltenango in order to elucidate the ways in which ideology impacted linguistic identification for some highland Maya women at the end of the twentieth century. This chapter calls into question accepted notions about Maya women's role in social reproduction by looking at the linguistic identification of young urban Kaqchikel women. It does so by transcending the indexical relation between linguistic conservatism and gender, so as to map out the ideologizing of such connections by various social actors, including North American anthropologists, Maya linguists, and Spanish-Kaqchikel bilingual Mayas involved in wage labor activities. The chapter argues that the current language shift from Kaqchikel to Spanish in many of these communities is a product and productive of local notions of "modern" personhood that are experienced differently by men and women.

Through these varied examples from K'iche' and Kaqchikel communities, I aim to demonstrate the ways in which conceptions of local identity contest and challenge absolute links between Mayan languages and the project of a collective Maya identity. These grassroots, alternative language ideologies illustrate forms of identification that are active in the imaginary of ordinary Maya citizens, yet absent from official state discourse and the discourse of Maya intellectuals. Furthermore, they reveal forms of collective identification that center around notions of "tradition" and "modernity" that have yet to enter into public discourse and have yet to be addressed by the Maya movement.

The final chapter, "Vernacular Modernities and the Objectification of Tradition," synthesizes the findings of previous chapters and argues further that modernity was the key trope assumed, negotiated, and reconfigured by the Maya movement and its interlocutors in early twenty-first century Guatemalan cultural and linguistic politics. It suggests that the strategic objectification of "tradition" is one of the key features of these vernacular modernities. In conclusion, I propose that it may become particularly important to consider objectifications of "tradition" of and by Maya peoples in increasingly *transnational* contexts, like tourism directed at North American and Western Europeans, international development efforts to represent "multiculturalism" in Guatemala, and immigration and human rights issues involving indigenous Maya peoples in the United States.

CHAPTER 1

The Paradox of Ethnolinguistic Identity
Essentialisms, State-Sponsored Violence, and Cultural Rights

CONSIDER THE FOLLOWING critical reflection on Maya culture in Guatemala:

> Los indígenas no pueden tener cultura, ya que son cerrados, analfabetos, atrasados y haraganes y encima de todo ladrones.
> [The Indians can't have culture, they are closed, illiterate, backward, lazy, and, on top of it all, thieves.] (Casaus Arzú 1992:274)

Now juxtapose it with this antithetical perspective:

> Xtik'atzin ta k'a chi ke ri taq ixtani' taq alab'o'
> ri e ral jäl, e ral ixim
> ruma pa kiq'a' rije' k'oj wi ri k'ak'a' rusaqarisab'äl ri Maya' Amaq'
> ruma chuqa' pa kiq'a' rije' k'oj wi ri rutzeqelib'exik ruk'aslem
> ri qach'abäl.[1]
> [To the boys and girls of the corn who are the future of the Maya people, because in their hands is the new radiant dawn of Maya culture and the continuation of Mayan languages.] (García Matzar and Rodríguez Guaján 1997:4).

The former is a commonplace conception of "Indian" identity articulated by a fifty-nine-year-old elite Ladina; the latter is a visionary book dedication to future guardians of Maya culture written by two Kaqchikel linguists. Taken together as emblematic, they underscore the importance of Maya culture in Guatemalan national discourse and highlight its contested meanings and locations. Their juxtaposition also indicates that objectified constructions of culture are implicated in essentialized notions of social difference, in this case indigenous identity (French 2008:109). As I outlined in the introduction, the issue of essentialist constructs of social difference, specifically Maya Indian and Ladino ones, has fundamentally structured Guatemalan national politics in the twentieth century. We can consider the oppositional constructions of an essentialized indigenous identity—one promoted by the state in service of the hegemonic and violent project to create a homogenous Guatemala, and one endorsed by the Maya movement in a self-conscious attempt to reconfigure the Guatemalan nation into a multicultural democracy—as two powerfully competing political projects. Both state-sponsored homogeneous nation-building efforts and Pan-Maya ethnonationalist cultural rights activism assume that Mayan languages are iconic representations of Maya peoples, as if Mayan languages "depicted or displayed the group's inherent nature or essence" (Irvine and Gal 2000:37).

The particular instances of essentialist ideologies of language in Guatemala are, in turn, indicative of similar ideological processes underway in a variety of multilingual, multiethnic nation-states (Blommaert and Verschueren 1998; Bokhorst-Heng 1999; Jaffe 1999; Errington 2000; Irvine and Gal 2000).[2] Indeed, as Woolard notes, this Herderian ideology of language linking a particular code with the essence of a unified people has become globally hegemonic today (1998:17). While several scholars of language have rightly challenged such essentializing ideologies by showing a diversity of linguistic ideologies circulating in a given ethnographic context (Urciuoli 1996; Gal 1998), less attention has been devoted to uncovering the ways in which such nationalist ideologies that are hegemonic become efficacious. Noting this lack, Woolard poses the following scholarly challenge: "Although the validity of the nationalist ideology of language (linking a language with a collective people) has often been debated or debunked, less attention has traditionally been given to understanding how the view of languages not only as discrete, distinctive entities but emblematic of self and community comes to take hold in so many different settings" (1998:18). Because the specific construction of essentialist ideologies of language in post-conflict Guatemala has yielded two oppositional political projects, the linking of Mayan languages with the essence of Maya peoplehood provides us with a unique opportunity to take up Woolard's suggested inquiry. Furthermore, this inquiry into how nationalist ideologies come to take hold in specific communities resonates with Bauman and Briggs's project to uncover how the institutions and agents of modernity (the nation-state and scientific experts) homogenize heterogeneous linguistic and social fields in ways that further inequality (2003). In the pages that follow, I aim to show some experiences and processes by which essentialist, hegemonic ideologies of language and collective identity have come to take hold among bilingual Kaqchikel communities in the latter half of the twentieth century. I argue that an essentialized ideology of Mayan languages as inherently emblematic of indigenous identity in bilingual Kaqchikel communities has been socialized through extreme violence propagated by the Guatemalan state, as well as creatively engendered through linguistic activism by Pan-Maya scholars seeking new forms of inclusion at the national level.

The Violence of Ethnolinguistic Identity

During the course of my ethnographic fieldwork in Guatemala among highland bilingual communities over the past fifteen years, it has become clear to me that Kaqchikel and K'iche' speakers' experiences of becoming bilingual in Spanish during the 1960s and 1970s are inextricably connected with La Violencia. Individuals' quotidian discourse about the process of acquiring Spanish highlights both the violent nature of the experiences and the omnipresence of the state as an agent of language change in their lives. Indeed, the forced measures and actions of the state's agents engendered what I call an "ideology of exclusivity"—a conception of language change in which the acquisition of Spanish is understood to be obtained at the expense of indigenous peoples' first languages. Consequently, when indigenous Kaqchikel and K'iche' people become imagined as monolingual Spanish speakers, their perceived linguistic assimilation is, from the essentialist and dominant perspective of the state, hegemonically conceptualized as a victory in erasing "Indian" identity for the good of the nation.[3]

I now turn to narratives told to me by Fidencio Kan during the spring of 1997 in Sumpango, Guatemala. As a bilingual Kaqchikel-Maya who came of age under repressive conditions imposed by the Guatemalan state, Fidencio Kan embodies a perspective representing that of many indigenous men living in urban environs who chose not to pass on their first language to their children. Fidencio Kan's "living memory of violence" (Sanford 2003) provides valuable insight into the experiences and ideologies underpinning language shift that are prevalent in most Kaqchikel and K'iche' highland communities (Richards 2003).

Don Fidencio grew up in a Kaqchikel monolingual household in the village of San Martín, Chimaltenango, the Kaqchikel community that was hardest hit by state-sponsored violence during the armed conflict and genocide. As with most life stories, his was also selectively remembered and told. During the ten years that I have known him, Don Fidencio has shared some definitive moments with me, not necessarily in chronological order. At some point in his youth, Don Fidencio left his village because he was conscripted into the army. While with the army in the K'iche' region of Quetzaltenango, he met and married his wife, a local indigenous K'iche' speaker from a rural *aldea* ("hamlet"). Together, they returned to urban Kaqchikel environs and rented a house within a predominantly Ladino town near the national capital, Guatemala City. During his adult life, Don Fidencio completed his high school–level education, involved himself in entrepreneurial activities (including tourism), and began to raise five monolingual Spanish children. Never did I hear or overhear Don Fidencio speak in Kaqchikel with his wife, his children, his coworkers, or fellow Catholics from his local parish in any quotidian context that I was privy to while living with the family; Spanish was Don Fidencio's unmarked code of daily use. Don Fidencio narrated his memories in Spanish, a fact intimately connected with violent consequences for speaking Kaqchikel (as we will see below) and a concomitant commitment to heading an exclusively monolingual Spanish household with the hopes of improving his children's futures.

As we consider the memories of forced military service, coercive literacy classes, and authoritarian state agents recounted in Don Fidencio's narratives, I want to underscore that my discussions with him centered on the seemingly benign topic of speaking Spanish and Kaqchikel. In other words, neither violence nor the state were discourse topics that I ever introduced into our conversations; in fact, it would have been extremely inappropriate of me to do so, given the perceived danger of mentioning such things for fear of reprisal (Green 1999). Rather, it is precisely because these themes emerged organically in the context of Don Fidencio's narratives about his experiences with the languages he spoke that my analytic focus on the relationships among indigenous identity, violence, and the state becomes tenable.

One afternoon, after I returned from my language lesson with a local Kaqchikel instructor and was studying at the family table, Don Fidencio arrived home and queried me politely, yet again, about my interest in learning Kaqchikel. I had the feeling that he couldn't quite make sense of why I would devote my mental and financial resources to studying the language. While Don Fidencio had explicitly endorsed my study of his natal language, he was also quick to point out that, in actuality, only a very few elderly people still spoke the language. In other words, he was indirectly questioning the utility of learning Kaqchikel:

1) DF: Ya es poca, poca gente [que habla Kaqchikel].
   Now it's very few, few people that speak Kaqchikel.
2) Ya es la gente anciana. Es la gente anciana,
   Now it is just the old people. It's the old people,
3) que ellos ya no se dedicaron, unas que otras palabras ellos
   those who didn't dedicate themselves, some words here and there that they
4) comprenden en castellano. Pero ya la mayor parte (1), fue ya en en año de,
   understand in Spanish. But now the majority, it was in the year,
5) (2.5), en el año cincuenta más o menos y empezó. Ya con, ya
   in the year 1950 more or less and it started. Now with, now
6) los gobernantes que empezaron a raíz de eso y se movilizó lo que es
   the rulers, they started the roots of this and that which is Spanish
7) el castellano. Porque, entonces, este gobierno autorizó, para no
   was mobilized. Because, so, this government authorized to not
8) hablar más en, en (2) idioma de (1), de orígenes,
   speak anymore in, in, the language of [one's] origins,
9) en las escuelas, solo español, español.
   in the schools, only Spanish, Spanish.
10) Fue ya directamente en la época de Carlos Castillo Armas.
    It was directly in the epoch of Carlos Castillo Armas.
11) Más o menos en los años sesenta que empezaron a prohibir todo esto.
    More or less in the sixties when they began to prohibit all of this.
12) Entonces ya, ya los niños empezaron a aprender
    So then, now the children began to learn
13) solo en castellano, castellano.
    only in Spanish, Spanish.
14) Y esto fue una evolución cuando floreció directamente de español.
    And this was an evolution when Spanish directly began to flourish.

15) Entonces, bajó lo que es directamente nuestro, nuestro lengua
   So, it declined that which is directly our, our, language
16) de orígenes. Bajó por completo.
   of origins. It declined completely.

In his efforts to explain to me the potential utility of Kaqchikel, Don Fidencio identifies with people who speak the language, marked by the indexical shifter (Silverstein 1976) "our" in line 15, even as he describes the transformation of Kaqchikel-speaking communities into Spanish ones as an "evolution" (line 14) with positive and progressive connotations, a point which is further underscored in the transcript that follows. While using eloquent formal discourse structures like parallelism (lines 9 and 13) and repetition (lines 1, 2, 9 and 13) commonly deployed in monolingual Maya speech to create authority and affect, Don Fidencio draws attention to the agent of language change in institutional terms. He names "the rulers" (line 6) and "the government" (line 7) as those responsible for instigating language change to Spanish in his natal Kaqchikel community. These state actors "authorized" the use of Spanish only in schools (line 7) and authored the concomitant prohibition of Kaqchikel (line 11). Don Fidencio's keen attention to the specific powerful agents in language change among Kaqchikel-Maya communities is further underscored when he names the "epoch of Carlos Castillo Armas" (line 10) as a transformational period in Kaqchikel communities.

Don Fidencio returns to bring up the presidency of Castillo Armas later in his narrative when he introduces another key feature of the violence of linguistic change—forced military service. As we will see, the ideology of exclusivity—namely, the relational linking of Spanish and Kaqchikel as mutually exclusive codes—emerges clearly in Don Fidencio's metalinguistic talk, an interpellation of state discourses revoiced in his own words. These themes of dictatorships and coercion unfold as Don Fidencio returns to emphasize the point that almost everyone in urban Kaqchikel communities now speaks Spanish:

17) DF: La mayor parte de los que no hablan [castellano] están en casa.
   The majority of those who don't speak [Spanish] stay at home.
18) Un tiempo (1), en el tiempo de Carlos Castillo Armas, estaría hablando
   One time, in the time of Carlos Castillo Armas, I'd be talking

19) del año, como el año (3) sesenta y ocho más o menos (3) Hubo
    about the year, around the year sixty-eight more or less . . . There was

20) esa época que fue obligatoriamente, todos los hombres, todos los varones
    this time when it was obligatory, all of the men, all of the males

21) tenían que prestar servicio militar.
    had to go into military service.

22) BF: ¿Todos?
    All of them?

23) DF: Sí todos, todo varón tenía que prestar obligatoriamente.
    Yes all of them, all males had to go into military service obligatorily.

24) En este tiempo, todo. Él que iba a servicio militar, les quitaban
    In this time, all of them. He who went into military service, they took

25) el hablante Kaqchikel o cualquier dialecto, y le incorporaban
    away the speakers' Kaqchikel or whatever dialect, and they incorporated

26) el castellano. Ya cuando regresaban a su (1), su tierra, ya les prohibían
    Spanish. When they returned to their, their land, now they prohibited them

27) hablar en, en, en Kaqchikel o otro idioma, sino que,
    to speak in, in, in Kaqchikel or another [Mayan] language, rather

28) *tenían que, ellos, ya fue uno como una (??) autoregulacíon*
    they had to, they, it was like a self-regulation

29) directamente en el hablante. Entonces, ahora ya no.
    directly with the speaker. So now, no [they don't speak in Kaqchikel.]

Don Fidencio's second mention of the Castillo Armas regime (line 18) underscores the authority of the Guatemalan state, an authority personified by the dictator who made military service obligatory for young indigenous men (lines 19–23). This forced military service is, in turn, directly linked to collective language change from Kaqchikel to Spanish, in which the speaker is situated as the object whose native language was stripped away and replaced with Spanish (lines 24–27) by state agents outside local Maya communities. Indeed, Castillo Armas was the military leader put in place by the CIA-sponsored coup of 1954, who ruled the nation until 1957 (Schlesinger and Kinzer 1999). His regime is particularly significant for inaugurating a series of military dictatorships that persisted in various forms during the thirty-six-year armed conflict. Yet, more than a simple and transparent recapitulation of historical "facts," Don Fidencio's narrative shows how the social memory of language and violence inhabits daily speech. Its legacy persisted after men completed their military service and returned to their communities because they were prohibited from speaking in Kaqchikel. Consequently, young men disciplined themselves to repress the language in their speech because of their experiences as conscripts (lines 26–29). This historic self-censorship among indigenous men returning from the army, much like Don Fidencio's daily practices decades later, recreates another form of violence—the symbolic violence of linguistic erasure. The linguistic erasure of Kaqchikel is based upon "the most effective and best concealed censorships that exclude certain agents from communication by excluding them from the groups which speak or the places which allow one to speak with authority" (Bourdieu 1991:138). Thus, Kaqchikel becomes excluded from much "authorized" public discourse among bilingual communities that were targets of state-sponsored violence. Adult Kaqchikel men's past experiences of forcible language change as conscripts in the Guatemalan military provide the very foundation for language ideologies that exclusively privilege Spanish among this group and their families at the end of the twentieth century.

Further experiences with state-mandated language change under the threat of violence—this time in the form of compulsory literacy classes—emerge in Don Fidencio's narrative. His discourse articulates the paradox of speaking Spanish for many bilingual Mayas who lived during La Violencia; Spanish is seen as both the product of force in the past and a benefit in the present for those who command it. In that way, Don Fidencio recreates the army's logic that benevolent violence can be used "to improve the Indian's way of life," (CEH 1999; Hale 2006:51), even as he was a victim of it.

30) DF: El gran recurso que tuvimos fue en el año 1980–86, que
     The great resource that we had was in the year 1980–86, when
31) fue obligatoriamente, tenían que asistir a alfabetización.
     it was obligatory, they had to attend literacy classes.
32) BF: ¿Sí?
     Really?
33) DF: Sí, esto fue obligatoriamente en el tiempo del gobierno del Lucas,
     Yes, it was obligatory in the time of the government of Lucas,
34) hasta incluso hubieron amanenzas para los que no asistían
     including that there were even threats against those who didn't attend
35) a esas clases.
     those classes.

36) BF: ¿En serio?
   Seriously?

37) DF: Sí. Por ejemplo sucede (2) sucede, por ejemplo, en mi pueblo,
   Yes. For example, what happens, happens, for example in my village

38) había mucha gente que no (1), que no tenían, que no,
   there were many people who didn't, who didn't have, who didn't,

39) no sabían leer. Ahora yo admiro que esa gente
   who didn't know how to read [in Spanish]. Now I admire that those people

40) ya sabe leer . . . porque decían, "El que no asistía
   now know how to read . . . because they said, "He who does not attend

41) a sus clases es porque es gente guerrillera." Entonces, para no sentir
   his classes because he is a guerilla." So, to not feel

42) esta acusación, tenían que ir forzosamente, ir a asistir a las clases.
   this accusation, they had to go against their will, go attend the classes.

43) A veces, hasta con los niños, con los niños, y tenían que aprender.
   Sometimes, even with the children, with the children, and they had to learn.

44) Allí prácticamente, ya estuvo borrando, borrando mucho lo que es
   From there on practically, it was already erasing, erasing, much of what is

45) nuestra idioma, porque fue forzosamente y directamente.
   our language, because it was coercive and direct.

In this section of Don Fidencio's narrative, his quotative discourse re-
voices the powerful social forces during the regime of President Lucas,
who literally threatened the lives of those people who did not attend
Spanish classes ("hubieron amanenzas" in line 34). The directly cited
military authority indexically links Spanish illiteracy with politically sub-
versive activity—as in "he . . . does not attend his [literacy] classes because
he is a guerilla" in lines 40 and 41—in such a way that the essential
construction of Indianness as antithetical to Guatemalan national identity is laid bare. In other words, if one speaks in Kaqchikel and not in
Spanish, one is perceived to be a danger to the nation—a danger created
by the recursive projection of linguistic difference onto social difference
(Irvine and Gal 2000)—that must be eradicated from the body politic of
the nation. In this way, forced literacy classes in Maya communities during the years of the repressive Lucas dictatorship (1978–1982) were yet
another way in which violence and the state were implicated in local
Kaqchikel communities' understandings of language ideologies and indigenous identity.

Don Fidencio's strong endorsement of the "positive" results of these violent processes is particularly significant for our understanding of how hegemonic ideologies of language come to take hold. Ultimately, he understands forced literacy classes under the threat of military action against civilians who did not attend as a "great resource" (line 30) for his community that produced results that he "admires" (lines 39–40). In effect, Don Fidencio's narrative entextualizes commonplace military propaganda. Indeed, his perspective is strikingly akin to that articulated by a military leader in Chimaltenango, who asserted that "the army is a great motor of integration that teaches indigenous people many valuable things" (Hale 2006:51). This ideology was used to justify actions taken against indigenous communities in the everyday lives of the survivors. As such, it becomes part of Don Fidencio's practical consciousness (Williams 1977) as a bilingual indigenous man who was conscripted by the army and who lived through the thirty-six-year civil war and genocide.

The specifics of Don Fidencio's narratives are, no doubt, particular to the lived understandings of language, violence, and identity that were experienced by men from the community of San Martín during the 1960s and 1970s. Nevertheless, similar experiences with language, identity, and violence are strikingly echoed in the testimonies of genocide survivors whose narratives were recorded by the United Nations–sponsored truth and reconciliation project, officially undertaken by the Commission for Historical Clarification (CEH) as part of the peace process. The final report of the CEH, *Guatemala: Memoria del silencio* (*Guatemala: Memory of Silence*)(1999), formally documented extensive human rights violations in Guatemala; analyzed the causes of violence, including the structural oppression of indigenous populations; and made recommendations for national reconciliation. An examination of survivor testimonies recorded in the CEH's report reveals the striking degree to which agents of the state explicitly sanctioned against speaking Mayan languages through the use of lethal violence against Maya peoples. For example, individuals from Popti' communities, an ethnolinguistic group with around thirty-two thousand speakers in the department of Huehuetenango, remembered the following:

46) Nos obligaron a dejar nuestro idioma y nuestros costumbres,
    They obliged us to leave our language and our customs,

47) decían que todo hombre que hablará en lengua era guerrillero,
   it was said all men who might speak in our language were guerrilla,
48) nos hicieron avergonzarnos de nuestras raíces para poder sobrevivir
   they made us become ashamed of our roots in order to survive.
   (Witness from Huista, Huehuetenango, CEH 1999:27)

As in Don Fidencio's narrative, the "we" of indigenous people is not constructed around a specifically named community, but instead around the "we" who were forcibly made to "leave our language and our customs" (line 46) in order to survive the state-sponsored violence. In other words, the collective "we" of ethnolinguistic identification is indexed negatively through a lack by those who were obliged to give up their natal languages so that they might live. In this instance, "they" refers to the army who threatened the lives of those who did not conform to non-Indian ways of culture and language. The ultimate example of the profound link between violence, language change, and indigenous identity among highland Maya communities is recounted in the testimony of another Popti' witness who testified to the CEH:

49) Algunas veces encontrábamos gente en la montaña pero como
   Sometimes we encountered people on the mountain, but because
50) no hablaban el castellano y nadie les entendía, ni el traductor
   they didn't speak Spanish and no one understood them, not even the
51) Jakalteko [Popti'] que llevábamos, el oficial nos daba
   Jakaltec translator that we had with us, the official gave us
52) el orden de matarlos.
   the order to kill them. (CEH 1999:187)

Here, we are faced with the ultimate material consequence of an essentialist construction of Indian identity based upon ethnolinguistic difference—murder. The official (line 51) is the agent who forced Maya people to kill other Mayas, literally and brutally instantiating the degree to which Indian identity was antithetical to belonging in the Guatemalan nation.

The Project of Maya Ethnolinguistic Identity

While such an essentialized understanding of Mayan languages and indigenous identity was a part of the productive conditions for the violent obliteration of Maya culture, it nevertheless has also been used productively to structure claims for some democratic social reform and multi-cultural nation-building in Guatemala during the post-conflict era. As I discussed in the introduction, the Maya movement seeks to create a Guatemalan nation reconstituted and redefined by the politics of cultural difference. This Maya cultural revitalization project, focused centrally (although not exclusively) on Mayan languages, is linked to the dual political objectives of promoting cultural autonomy for Maya peoples and reconfiguring the Guatemalan nation into a multilingual and multi-cultural democracy.

Central to the pursuit of the Maya movement's goals for cultural self-determination and progressive political reform within the Guatemalan state is the strategically essential linking of Mayan languages with the ideal of a unified Maya pueblo (people/nation) (French 1999). In other words, Mayan languages hold a unique place among several aspects of culture that are objectified as the fundamental essences of Maya identity —the very foundation upon which a collective Maya identity is erected. Dr. Demetrio Cojtí articulates the link between Mayan languages and Maya peoplehood as an essential one, as do most educated Maya schol-ars and activists professionally involved in cultural rights efforts. In a now canonized essay on Mayan linguistics, Cojtí defines Maya identity through a strategically essential claim: "The Maya people exist because they have and speak their own languages" (1990:12). This essentialist lan-guage ideology, linking Mayan languages with the ideal of collective Maya people in a nationalist sense, has acted as an effective means for structuring particular notions of difference and for legitimizing specific calls for cultural autonomy like those most recently rendered visible in the Ley de Idiomas Nacionales.

The demand that cultural rights be granted to a collective group by the state, such as the linguistic rights of Maya people, requires a prior foundation of an essential understanding of collective identity. The boundedness of that collective identity is most often conceptualized as the objectified "culture" that unifies a social group as a distinct people (Handler 1988; Domínguez 1989; Légaré 1995). Much like Maya ethno-nationalists, indigenous peoples throughout Latin America are struggling to articulate similar kinds of cultural rights claims based upon notions of difference for democratic social reform (Van Cott 1994; Warren and Jackson 2002; Yashar 2005). These myriad struggles make evident the fact that it is not enough for interested groups to solely assert, that is to say, *presuppose* essential cultural difference. Social actors and institutions must also actively *create* a difference that unifies identities in an essential way in order to warrant the pursuit of cultural rights claims. How then, have Maya scholars actively produced an essentializing project around ethnolinguistic identity for more inclusive ends at the national level?

To examine one of the ways in which Mayan languages are effectively mobilized for the project of engendering a collective Maya identity, I now return to the issue with which I began the book—namely, the Mayan languages officialization project and the linguistic ideological work entailed by the standardization efforts it involved. My discursive examination of a neologism project undertaken by the Kaqchikel Cholchi' (the Kaqchikel Linguistic Community) will show how Maya linguists constitute a distinct and essential Maya peoplehood through three interrelated aspects: (1) an invocation of a common history as indigenous people in Guatemala; (2) a Whorfian construction of "the" Maya worldview; and (3) a self-conscious emphasis on linguistic unification through the erasure of dialect variation within Kaqchikel, as well as the minimization of language variation within the diverse family of twenty-one Mayan languages spoken in Guatemala. As with narratives of language and violence analyzed earlier, here, too, the state is situated in Pan-Maya discourse as a primary actor in the process of shaping Maya ethnolinguistic identity in the past and present.

Language prescription, or the establishment of standards—particularly in written usage—has come to take on an important role in Maya cultural rights activism among indigenous linguists in Guatemala (England 1996:178 and 2003). The written codification of Mayan languages through standardization is deemed politically urgent in the case of Maya ethnonationalism precisely because standard written forms can function productively as an act of linguistic consolidation that can be recursively projected (Irvine and Gal 2000) onto collective identity consolidation. Indeed, this is the very process that Anderson (1991) assumes in his theoretical account of nationalism and Schieffelin and Doucet (1994) enumerate in their analyses of national identity formation: first, the commonplace ideology that language standardization enables linguistic unification;

second, that linguistic unification can provide the means by which print technologies circulate the written word that "re-presents the kind of imagined community that is national" (Anderson 1991:25).

Rukemik K'ak'a' Taq Tzij (Criteria for the Creation of Neologisms en Kaqchikel) is one aspect of the standardization project and one of myriad interventions meant to further *activate* the project of a strategically essential understanding of Maya ethnolinguistic identity. Kaqchikel Cholchi' directed the project in conjunction with the Mayan Languages Academy of Guatemala and with international funding and support from the United Nations Children's Fund (UNICEF). Several linguists— Kab'lajuj Tijax, Ixq'anil, Ixchayim, Pakal B'alam, Tz'unun Ya', Lolmay, and Raxche'—undertook the project with the explicit intention of helping to materialize new linguistic and cultural rights in Guatemala, including the right to an education in indigenous languages (Kaqchikel Cholchi' 1995:6), a right that was subsequently codified in the Ley de Idiomas Nacionales. How, then, do Kaqchikel-speaking linguists actively engender a collective unification of many distinct Maya communities as one Maya people through their linguistic work? As we will see below, a distinct peoplehood defined by and through Mayan languages is strategically constituted in the linguistic analysis of Kaqchikel neologisms.

In their theoretical introduction to criteria for creating neologisms, linguists begin their analysis by calling attention to the pre-Columbian history of Kaqchikel communities, as well as to the colonial history of domination that all Maya communities were subjected to in Guatemala.

53) Antes de 1524, el idioma Maya Kaqchikel tenía la categoría del único
    Before 1524, the Mayan language Kaqchikel had the status as the only
54) idioma de la Comunidad Lingüística que ahora conocemos como Maya
    language of the linguistic community that we now know as Maya
55) Kaqchikel. . . . Tanto los gobernados, como los gobernantes
    Kaqchikel. . . . The governed as well as the governors
56) tenían el mismo idioma de comunicación.
    had the same language of communication. (Kaqchikel Cholchi 1995:9)

Here, linguists hearken back to a pre-Columbian era when Kaqchikel-speaking Mayas were unified as one collective group. The indexical relationship between the Kaqchikel language and the Kaqchikel people is taken to be iconic ("Kaqchikel had the status as the only language of the linguistic community" in lines 53 and 54). In other words, the borders of a language and a people are ideologically configured as transparently iso-morphic in the historical era before Spanish colonialism came to subordi-nate both.

In their analysis, linguists highlight the drastic change produced by the history of colonialism for Kaqchikel-speaking communities. They then generalize this change as a unifying principle for the history of all Maya peoples in Guatemala, downplaying the vast differences in re-sponses to and impacts of the Spanish invasion among indigenous com-munities in Guatemala (Lutz 1984; Smith 1990a).

57) Al inicio del colonialismo sobre el Pueblo Maya en general y del
   In the beginning of colonialism over the Maya people in general and
58) Kaqchikel en particular, los ámbitos de uso del Kaqchikel se
   Kaqchikel [people] in particular, the contexts of Kaqchikel usage were
59) restringieron drásticamente. No fue más el idioma oficial,
   drastically limited. No longer was Kaqchikel the official language
60) del estado al ser destruido el Estado Kaqchikel.
   of the state as the Kaqchikel state was destroyed. (Kaqchikel Cholchi 1995:10)

As linguists craft a shared history of linguistic oppression among Maya peoples, they, like the individual Mayas in bilingual highland communi-ties whose narratives I analyzed earlier, draw attention to the significant role of the state in structuring officially sanctioned uses of Mayan lan-guages (line 60). From the linguists' perspective, Maya communities must both rely upon and return to their shared pre-Columbian indepen-dence and political power when they commanded the state (line 60). The privileging of an independent, shared history of Maya peoples is also central to linguists' contemporary choices in selecting the specific stan-dard forms that they put forth in their linguistic projects. Nora England explains: "Historical 'authenticity' has become a criterion of substantial weight [in choosing among competing forms for standardization]. For instance, showing that one form is 'older' than another may be enough to guarantee its acceptance" (2003:736). Here, the emphasis on older forms of language activates the notion of a deep cultural continuity in Maya identity from pre-Columbian times to the end of the twentieth century, an intervention that erases a long history of conflict among Maya groups during the pre-Columbian and colonial eras.

In addition to the active construction of a shared and unifying history among Maya peoples, linguists' analysis in Rukemik K'ak'aka Taq Tzij produces a strategically essential Maya ethnolinguistic identity by emphasizing a uniquely Maya worldview. In particular, they stress the "inherent" relationship between the Kaqchikel lexicon and Maya *cosmovisión*, invoking what they refer to as an explicitly "anthropological" understanding of language. These linguists link vocabulary and worldview in the following way:

61) Por medio del vocabulario se transmiten conceptos o significados de
   Through vocabulary, concepts or meanings are transmitted that are
62) acuerdo a la cultura. . . . Los idiomas de origen maya tienen
   in accordance with the culture. . . . The languages of Mayan origin have
63) inmerso dentro de su vocabulario cosmovisión.
   immersed in their vocabulary cosmovision. (Kaqchikel Cholchi 1995:14)

Their linguistic analysis goes on to specify the importance of nouns that embody a uniquely metaphysical Maya perception of the world:

64) Es decir, que el vocabulario hace referencia a que todos
   That is to say, that the vocabulary makes reference to all
65) los elementos del universo están interrelacionados así como una sola
   the elements of the universe that are interrelated like a single
66) energía. Los Mayas vemos los elementos de la naturaleza con vida al
   energy. We the Mayas see the elements of nature with life
67) igual que humano.
   equal to that of human [life]. (1995:14)

In this instance of linguistic analysis, "the" Maya perception of the universe as a living organism made up of anthropomorphic elements (lines 66–67) is ideologically crafted into the basis of a collective, unified Maya peoplehood. From this perspective, all Mayas ("We the Mayas," line 66) who transmit the languages are situated as interconnected on the metaphysical and linguistic planes. In other words, a distinctly Whorfian understanding of language and worldview is marshaled for political ends. The examples below demonstrate the active configuration of a uniquely and essentially Maya cosmovisión instantiated through the linguistic analysis of neologisms. This principle of Maya cosmovisión is actively drawn upon in the creation of neologisms to further unify speakers—to find shared "old ways" of naming new concepts, thereby attempting to unify past and present Maya peoples into one imagined community. Some examples are demonstrated in three proposed neologisms below:

68) kajulew = universe:
   /kaj/ (sky) + /ulew/ (land)
69) ik'ch'umil = astronomy:
   /ik'/ (moon) + /ch'umil/ (star)
70) kematz'ib' = computer:
   /kem/ (a weaving) + /a/ (connects to roots) + /tz'ib'/ (writing)

Like the Xavante's creative use of new words used in service of indigenous activism in Brazil, Kaqchikel neologisms for concepts like universe, astronomy, and computer enable indigenous scholars and activists to "draw on elements from the discursive fields of the national and international arenas into which they increasingly move. This incorporation enables Indians to take part in the debates and discussions of those areas" (Graham 2002:212). In this way, neologisms serve to define an historically grounded Maya ethnolinguistic identity within distinctly modern, cosmopolitan national and international contexts from which they have been frequently excluded.

Linguists preferentially sanction linguistic homogenization over dialect heterogeneity in spoken discourse through their perspective on Spanish borrowings that indigenous neologisms may replace. This is the third facet of the manner in which Maya scholars actively attempt to consolidate a strategically essential ethnolinguistic identity around Kaqchikel and other Mayan languages. These analysts focus on the importance of creating neologisms explicitly for the project of standardization. As we will see, this standardization is implicitly linked to an ideology of purism that is presumed to strengthen the Maya nation.

71) Al fortalecer el vocabulario Kaqchikel, se está apoyando
   When we strengthen the Kaqchikel vocabulary, the process of
72) el proceso de estandarización, mediante la ampliación
   standardization is being supported through the amplification
73) del vocabulario del idioma. Con ello se impulsa
   of the vocabulary of the language. With it, the
74) la unidad lingüística de los hablantes kaqchikeles,
   linguistic unity of Kaqchikel speakers is driven forward,

75) al tener un mismo vocabulario para hacer referencia
    because there is a common vocabulary to make reference
76) a los avances científicos, tecnológicos, etc.
    to scientific, technological, and other advances. (1995:13)

The advancement of linguistic homogenization to unify Kaqchikel speakers in their references to new aspects of culture (lines 75–76) is, in turn, self-consciously extended outward to other Mayan languages. For example, the specific process for creating neologisms outlined by linguists in Rukemik K'ak'a' Taq Tzij includes new lexemes created from the following procedures: composition based upon the combination of roots, semantic extension, phonetic symbolism, and derivation (1995:18). The authors propose that the components of this productive methodology

77) guíen el trabajo lingüístico para la potencialización de
    guide the linguistic work for the growth of
78) los idiomas K'iche', especialmente el Kaqchikel. Así mismo, consideramos
    the K'iche'an languages, especially Kaqchikel. At the same time, we
79) que estos criterios, con las adaptaciones pertinentes
    consider that these criteria, with pertinent adaptations,
80) pueden ser utilizados por todos los idiomas Mayas.
    can be utilized by all Mayan languages. (Kaqchikel Cholchi 1995:12)

Thus, the principles of creating neologisms in Kaqchikel are understood as part of the larger language standardization project for the historically related languages in the K'iche' group of the Mayan family—which also include K'iche', Sipakapense, Sakapulteko, and Tz'utujiil ethnolinguistic groups that shared up to 85 percent of their vocabulary until the 1500s (1995:9). Maya linguists propose that the methodology for the creation of neologisms for standardization be extended to more distantly related Mayan languages with "pertinent adaptations" (line 79) for the project of linguistic unification of Maya peoples.

An ideology of linguistic purism is implicitly at work in the project of engendering a strategic Maya ethnolinguistic identity through the creation of neologisms used for standardization. Maya linguists rely on a formal, polite style associated with oratory to draw attention to the importance of purism for Mayan languages and people through *indirection* (Brody 1991; Brown 1993). The language analysts define and discuss comparative cases of linguistic borrowing, diglossia, and bilingualism from a variety of historical contexts, including French lexical and grammatical influence on English during the Norman occupation of England. They are quick to acknowledge that "no languages develop in a vacuum or in isolation" and that "language contact is a naturally occurring process" (Kaqchikel Cholchi' 1995:74). Nevertheless, Maya language analysts call attention to the macro-political contexts in which such linguistic phenomena occur. They conclude their discussion of "borrowings" with the following strong claim: "If the borrowing of words comes accompanied with social oppression, unstable/displacing diglossia, and asymmetrical bilingualism, it leads to the scenario of *linguacide*" (Kaqchikel Cholchi' 1995:78, emphasis in original).[4]

Taken together, Kaqchikel-speaking linguists actively constitute a strategically essential Maya ethnolinguistic identity through their analysis of neologisms by means of a notion of shared pre-Columbian and colonial histories of Maya peoples and languages, the Whorfian worldview embodied in them, and the great need for linguistic standardization and purification, in order to unite their speakers as a people. Such scholarly interventions are not merely esoteric. The Kaqchikel neologisms created by linguists figured prominently in a special issue of *Iximulew* (the neologism for Guatemala), a bilingual periodical that was printed in Spanish and a different Mayan language each month and was circulated nationally in the country's largest newspaper, *Siglo Veintiuno*, during the last decade of the twentieth century. The December 1996 issue of *Iximulew* (see fig. 2) was devoted to the proposed officialization of Mayan languages, highlighting the Kaqchikel Linguistic Community's innovative "linguistic engineering" (1996:7). Obdulio Son's essay, written in Spanish with an abstract in Kaqchikel, included an alphabetized list of eighty Kaqchikel neologisms with their Spanish translations. Son underscored that the lack of written forms of contemporary Mayan languages is a situation that favors monolingualism in Spanish (1996:7), thereby encouraging an ideology of linguistic purism put forth by linguists that is not salient in many contemporary Maya-speaking communities (Richards 1998; Reynolds 2002; Choi 2003; Brody 2004).

Referentially, new concepts represented in Kaqchikel neologisms "express creative engagements with the global world in which Indians now find themselves" (Graham 2002:212). However, in a country where literacy in Spanish is widely variable—from 15 percent in some areas to

Figure 2. "The Officialization of Mayan Languages: Challenges and Perspectives," a feature story by Obdulio Son appearing in the Maya periodical *Iximulew* (courtesy Centro de la Cultura Maya, Cholsamaj, and *Siglo Veintiuno*).

92 percent in others (Richards 2003)—and where literacy in Mayan languages is only now nascent among the most educated indigenous populations in the post-peace-accords era, the productivity of Kaqchikel neologisms circulating in national print media like *Iximulew* may lie in their iconic and indexical valiancy. In other words, regardless of the questionable levels of referential comprehension by Mayas and Ladinos alike, the

image of Kaqchikel as a written, codified, and publicly circulating language iconically embodies a perceptual and ideological sameness with Spanish. The iconization of Kaqchikel with Spanish, in turn, functions indexically to mark the new ways in which Kaqchikel becomes a "modern" language fit for a multicultural nation.

This example of linguistic analysis used to propose Kaqchikel neologisms shows how, as Bauman and Briggs argue, expert knowledge is a central component of producing the essentialized "one-nation-one-language ideology, that a common language is the social glue that bind[s] a people together, engenders a shared culture, and is a requisite for a viable state" (2003:302). In the case of post-conflict Guatemala, Kaqchikel linguists actively reproduce the same nationalist ideology of language to highlight cultural difference that the state violently used against indigenous Maya citizens to eradicate cultural difference from the body politic of the nation. The twentieth-century history of linguistic analysis, as it has been mobilized by both the state and the Pan-Maya movement for competing nationalist ends based upon ethnolinguistic identity projects, is further examined in the following chapter. As we will continue to see, these political efforts by both the state and the Pan-Maya movement structure various inclusions and exclusions of indigenous Maya people.

CHAPTER 2

Political Linguistics

*Expert Linguists and Modernist Epistemologies
in the Guatemalan Nation*

As I OUTLINED in the last chapter through a discussion of Kaqchikel neologisms, linguistic analysis can be mobilized for political ends. In the twentieth-century Guatemalan context, even phonemes became politically charged representations. Despite these links to the political, a good deal of anthropological and linguistic scholarship commonly defines a phoneme, in purely analytic terms, as a unit that objectively describes meaningful sounds within a particular linguistic code. Indeed, several different intellectual traditions in the study of human language focus on the necessity of accurate, objective, and analytic characterizations of human speech sounds. In the tradition of American anthropology, Franz Boas highlighted the importance of overcoming analysts' misapprehension of meaningful sounds in non-European languages (1889). Prague school linguists dedicated analyses to ascertaining the presence or absence of constituent "distinctive features" of phonemes (Trubetzkay [1939] 1969). French structural linguistics, following Ferdinand de Saussure, highlighted the importance of analyzing each phoneme as "the sum of the auditory impressions and articulatory movements, the unit heard and the unit spoken" (Saussure 1959:40) and initially foregrounded phonetics as linguistic science's preferred object of diachronic study (Saussure 1959:140). From several scholarly perspectives, then, a phoneme is perceived to be a descriptive tool for identifying language structure, rather than a political device for structuring social relations among unequal groups.

However, Bauman and Briggs remind us that modern scholarly analyses of language, like the analysis of sound and sound systems under particular consideration here, are, in fact, modes of social definition (2003:315). This perspective, coupled with my experiences listening to Maya linguists' decade-long disagreements about the number of vowels in K'iche', makes me confident that phonemes are political acts of representation. In fact, the study of grammar, like all analyses of phonemes, morphemes, and syntax, can never be purely descriptive and analytically objective— these units of language are specific acts of representation situated in particular contexts of production that involve inequality. For example, in Guatemala, most Ladinos and informally educated Mayas commonly refer to Mayan languages as *lenguas* (literally "tongues") and *dialectos* ("dialects") lacking in grammar, in stark contrast to Spanish, referred to as an *idioma* ("language") with a complete and complicated grammatical structure. As such, Maya linguists' and their secular North American counterparts' contemporary efforts to descriptively map the grammatical intricacies of Mayan languages, including their sounds, is an act of resistance to the systematic devaluation of Maya peoples and cultures. Their linguistic analyses are done with the hope of creating a more inclusive Guatemalan social order to replace the one that has marginalized indigenous people. The overtly politicized perspective on linguistic analysis is passionately articulated in Demetrio Cojtí's now-canonized essay on Mayan linguistics:

> There is no place for a neutral, objective, pure or apolitical linguistics. In this country, the linguist who works on Mayan languages only has two options: active complicity with prevailing colonialism and linguistic assimilation or activism in favor of a new linguistic order in which equality and rights for all languages is concretized, which implies equality and rights for the nations and peoples. (1991:19)[1]

While Cojtí and his colleagues embrace the political situatedness of linguistics in Guatemala, the general assumption that language can and should be the object of descriptive science continues to guide much contemporary linguistic inquiry in other contexts (Taylor 1990).[2] Emphasizing the perceived contemporary need for descriptive objectivity in the study of language, Taylor remarks, we "turn to trained professionals with specialist techniques: to descriptive linguists. . . . If properly performed, (descriptive) metalinguistic discourse is seen to be an empirical science, with truth (as opposed to political power) as its only authority" (1990:10). From this perspective, the linguist, as legislator, is expected to define and describe human languages in technical ways that serve to keep language abstracted and autonomous from social, economic, and political concerns and contexts (Bauman and Briggs 2003:305).

Extending further the link between linguistic analysis and ideology, several scholars (Silverstein 1998; Woolard 1998; Irvine and Gal 2000) have recently argued that all metalinguistic discourse, including the scholarly analysis of language, is situated in a larger socio-political field and is always impacted by ideology. For these anthropologists, the key question about linguistics is not how linguistic analysis may be related to objectivity, but rather how a belief in the scientific nature of linguistics comes to take hold as an efficacious regime of knowledge in a given historical and ethnographic context. Or, to put it in Bauman and Briggs's (2003) terms, to raise the questions: What are the circumstances under which Mayan languages became modern objects of scientific knowledge? And how does the concomitant metadiscursive regime of Mayan linguistics inscribe categories of ethnic and national difference?

I wish to take up these questions through an examination of the emergence and transformation of linguistic analysis as an authoritative field of knowledge mobilized in the construction of essentialist ethnic and national identities for different political projects in Guatemala from the 1920s to the mid-1980s. In other words, I will trace the successful rise of the "science" of linguistics with a necessary "eye to the conditions that enabled it and the social interests inscribed in it" (Errington 2001:20). Because the scientific advent of linguistics in Guatemala implicates the scholarly analysis of linguistic forms with larger political debates about national identity consolidation, my examination will rely on Gal's position that "scholarly arguments about linguistic problems are simultaneously coded contests that propose to define the nation . . . and claims to professional expertise that can legitimately provide such definitions" (1995:156). Following Gal's excellent analysis of linguistic debates and nation-building in eighteenth-century Hungary, I will attend to the emergence of linguistic analysis as an authoritative enterprise by focusing on the tripartite relationship between linguistic analysis, the social actors who position themselves as the legitimate purveyors of expert knowledge, and the process of national identity formation. Extending my study beyond Gal's work, I will focus this inquiry on the epistemological distinction between expert analysts and "native speakers," a division, I argue, that

authorizes a particular construction of "scientific" linguistics with political implications for national inclusions and exclusions.

Certainly there is a rich and complicated history of colonial linguistics of indigenous Latin American languages (Mannheim 1984; Errington
2001). The Spanish Crown's and priests' language ideologies about indigenous languages were quite ambivalent and produced "zigzagging shifts
in orientation" (Mannheim 1984:294). Because my purpose here is to
show the ways in which linguistic analysis becomes implicated in explicitly modernist projects, I frame this inquiry around three historical
moments in the contemporary nation-building era to demonstrate the
shifting configurations of ideologies of language and their linking with
forms of ethnolinguistic belonging produced by differently positioned
social actors. First, I discuss U.S. missionary linguists, who produced early
twentieth-century grammars of Kaqchikel and whose claim to expert authority rested on their explicit goal of assimilating native speakers of
Mayan languages into the imagined Guatemalan national community
and the Christian faith through Spanish. Second, I examine the professionalization of linguistics as a scholarly discipline in Guatemala during
the 1950s. I show how Evangelical missionary linguists of the Summer
Institute of Linguistics and scholars associated with the National Indigenous Institute in Guatemala struggled to control the linguistic analysis
of Mayan languages. They aligned their "scientific" endeavors with the
state's efforts to forge a homogeneous national identity, a national identity
based upon the erasure of cultural and linguistic difference. Finally, I
conclude with an examination of Maya linguists' struggles during the
violence and post-violence eras to reconstitute expert knowledge and to
realign the scientific direction of linguistic analysis with their larger political struggle to engender a multicultural, multiethnic, and multilingual
Guatemalan nation.

Through an examination of these three historical moments, I show
that the powerful link between expert linguistic analysis and interested
definitions of the nation hinges on assumptions about and orientations
toward "native speakers" of Mayan languages. I argue that so long as
"native speakers" remain the object of dominant language assimilation
and are understood to have "limited awareness" of the complex grammatical structures of their languages, claims of expertise function to

naturalize the authority of the expert analyst and to establish hegemonic, exclusive definitions of the nation. However, an understanding of recent efforts by Maya linguists shows that when the assumption of a mutually exclusive epistemological division between "expert linguist" and "native speaker" is challenged, linguistic analysis and its claims to scientific expertise can be used for the purpose of promoting alternative versions of the imagined national community that strive to be more inclusive.

Grammars, God, and the Guatemalan Nation

The history of contemporary linguistic analysis of Mayan languages in Guatemala during the early twentieth century may very well begin with the work of W. Cameron Townsend, the founder of the Summer Institute of Linguistics (SIL), also known as the Wycliffe Bible Translators, in the early 1920s.[3] Townsend began his career and international evangelical project in 1919 as an ambulatory Bible-vendor-turned-proselytizer among Kaqchikel speakers in the Guatemalan highland communities of Patzún, San Antonio Aguas Calientes, and Comalapa (Stoll 1982). As Townsend became more involved in and committed to spreading Christianity in these Kaqchikel areas, he became troubled that new congregations in Maya communities "were springing up around poorly apprehended Spanish Bibles" (Stoll 1982:36). Convinced of the need to more clearly and efficiently spread the word of God in the local language, Townsend took a keen interest in the structure of Kaqchikel. Soon after, in 1926, he completed its first twentieth-century grammar.[4]

Townsend's *Cakchiquel Grammar* examines some grammatical patterns of the Kaqchikel language, including phonetics, and provides descriptive analyses of morphology, verbal prefixes, possessive pronominal prefixes, root stems, gender specific suffixes, and verbal suffixes.[5] For Townsend, understanding Kaqchikel morphology was the key to understanding the true "nature" of the language, a language he characterized as based upon primitive roots (1961:12). Conflating grammatically "basic" roots with politically "primitive" ones, Townsend argued that the essence of Kaqchikel would be iconically revealed as one learned the "primitive" roots and the corresponding inflections and derivations of Kaqchikel prefixes and suffixes. On the basis of this linguistic ideology linking "primitive" language with productive morphology, Townsend constructed a "slot-class tagmemic theory" of Kaqchikel in which morphemes were categorized according to productive classes. For example, Townsend analyzes the utterance "Xquebencamisabextaj–ka–na–can," glossed as "with an instrument I will go to kill them rapidly—in reference to a downward movement, and in reference to something expected and finished by that act, I will leave" in the following manner:

Xqu–e–be–n–cam–isa–be–xta–j–ka–na–can

Xqu   future time

e   third-person plural of substantive verb, indicating that the objective is plural and third person

be   the verb "to go," indicating that the agent will go away in order to act

n   abbreviation of the pronominal possessive prefix "nu," indicating that the agent is singular and in first person

cam   verb root signifying "to die"

isa   causative suffix

be   instrumental suffix

xta   rapid movement suffix

j   indicator of active voice

ka   auxiliary verb indicating action in downward direction

na   auxiliary verb indicating necessary action

can   enclitic indication that the action is finished or left or abandoned (Townsend cited in Pike 1961:4).

Townsend explained the significance of his morphemic analysis in the following way:

> The number of root words in the language is very small, but an almost unlimited number of derivatives can be formed by the use of prefixes and suffixes. Get thoroughly acquainted with the prefixes and suffixes and learn the root words and the language will be easy. One can understand words he has never heard before merely by recognizing the root and the suffix. (1961:9)

The explicit purpose Townsend assigned to this type of morphological analysis was to enable non-Mayas, particularly U.S. missionaries, to learn Kaqchikel efficiently, in order to spread Spanish and Christianity among monolingual speakers of Kaqchikel. SIL linguists eventually praised

Townsend's method for its applicability to many other indigenous American languages (Pike 1961; SIL 2000), and several SIL staff produced grammatical analyses of Mayan and other indigenous American languages that focused on the tagmeme as the unit of analysis (Church and Church 1961; Delgaty 1961; Elliott 1961; Pike 1982).

In Townsend's morphological (as well as phonetic and syntactic) descriptions, the semiotic processes of iconization—the transfer of an indexical relationship between language and a linked feature into a relationship perceived to be inherent—and erasure—the simplification of a linguistic field rendering some aspects invisible (Irvine and Gal 2000:37–38)—are at work. While Irvine and Gal underscore the importance of iconization and erasure in the construction of linguistic and social difference, in Townsend's work, these aspects function antithetically to produce a perceptual *sameness* between Kaqchikel and Spanish. One of several examples can be seen in Townsend's description of the "state of being" verb in Kaqchikel, which he conjugated as:

First-person singular	yin	First-person plural	oj
Second-person singular	at	Second-person plural	ix
Third-person singular	ja	Third-person plural	e (or je)

Stressing an isomorphic relationship between Kaqchikel and Spanish, Townsend remarked: "Like soy, eres, es, etc. in Spanish, these forms do not require the use of the nominative pronouns but may take them if desired" (1961:13). This recurring analytic perspective relies on the erasure of substantive grammatical differences between Kaqchikel and Spanish in order to produce an essential similarity between the languages.

Emphasizing the inherent "sameness" of the languages through grammatical description was the first step in facilitating Kaqchikel speakers' acquisition of literacy in Spanish, as epitomized in the progression of Townsend's linguistic and religious projects. Townsend produced a biblical translation of the New Testament fourteen years after he began studying and describing Kaqchikel (Hvalkof and Aaby 1981:9). It was a version of the Bible that he believed "would help Indians acquire the more prestigious, advantageous tongue, whereupon parents would raise their children as Spanish speakers" (Stoll 1982:37). This assimilationist orientation functioned to erase linguistic differences between Kaqchikel and

Spanish in order to erase social differences between "Indians" and Ladinos. As I outlined in the introduction and demonstrated in the previous chapter, such attempts at erasing social and cultural differences between "Indians" and "non-Indians" in the service of Guatemalan nation building had been an explicit part of the state goal of creating a homogenous nation from the mid-nineteenth century until the late twentieth century (Smith 1990b).

Indeed, the first definite signs of an explicit link between linguistic analysis and an interested version of nation building appeared in President Orellana's commendation of Townsend's missionary presence in Guatemala (Stoll 1982:31) and in the concomitant governmental support of SIL expertise in the analysis of Mayan languages.[6] This link between politics and linguistics characterized the type of analysis that dominated the intellectual scene from the 1920s until the mid-1950s. It came to be challenged eventually and gradually by "native speakers" of Mayan languages.

The earliest challenge was issued by the work of two Maya groups formed in 1945 that offered an alternative manner of linking linguistic analysis and collective identity formation. The Convención de Maestros Indígenas (Convention of Indigenous Teachers) and Academia de la Lengua Maya Ki-ché (ALMK) stressed Maya participation in linguistic analysis and implicated linguistics with the maintenance of Mayan languages in an increasingly adversarial national climate. Adrián Chávez, a K'iche'-Maya and a central figure in both of these organizations, argued for the development of an orthography that would represent the uniqueness of Mayan languages. Underscoring the essential difference between Mayan languages and Spanish, Chávez explained the need for a truly "Mayan" orthography: "[There is] the need to make a correction in the K'iche' manuscript for which it was advisable to use a set of symbols genuinely indigenous to bring out the marvelous beauty of the old culture" (Ministerio de Educación 1985:123).[7] Writing against existing SIL Spanish-like orthographies, Chávez developed one he called distinctly Mayan, using twenty-seven graphemes (nineteen from the Spanish orthography, one from English orthography, and seven "new" symbols). Although Chávez' orthography was used only in ALMK-published materials, it marked an important moment in Mayan linguistics generally, and Mayan language phonetics and their graphemic representation specifically. It highlighted Mayas' conviction in the essential difference of

Mayan languages from the official and national language, Spanish, as well as Mayas' interest in iconically realizing this difference in written forms.

Even though these two Maya groups contested linguistic representations of Mayan languages, it would take a few decades until Maya linguists developed themselves into an oppositional force that could effectively contest the direction of linguistics in the country. Nevertheless, these groups set the stage for subsequent Maya groups, linguists, and activists in the 1970s and 1980s to challenge the dominant ideology that guided SIL and the state. As we will see, it was in the 1970s that linguistic analysis became a site of struggle by two competing forces that mobilized it toward two distinct ends—linguistic assimilation to Spanish and language revitalization of Mayan languages. For those on both sides of this struggle, the analytic capacity and participation of the "native speaker" of Mayan languages was central.

Fixating on Phonetics:
The Politics and Semiotics of Sounds

While a few Mayas began to train as teachers and to take a formal interest in Mayan linguistics, the Guatemalan state secured even further SIL's authority over that domain. The government created a new institution, the Instituto Indigenista Nacional (IIN), in 1945. The explicit mission of the IIN was to "develop the scientific investigation of the country's ethnic groups to successfully achieve their promotion and integration into the national culture and to carry out studies of the country's indigenous languages for their literacy [in Spanish] and castillianization" (López 1989:31). Together, IIN staff, in conjunction with SIL linguists who were contracted to work with them (Hvalkof and Aaby 1981), pursued the goal to control representations of Mayan languages for the purpose of cultural and religious assimilation of Maya populations, namely, to transform "Indians" into literate Christian Guatemalans.

Collaboration between the IIN and SIL was precipitated in the Primer Congreso de Lingüística (First Linguistic Congress) in 1949, sponsored by the Ministry of Education. The meeting's primary objective was to deal with the problem of "multiple forms of graphic representation for the indigenous languages of the country" (IIN 1950:5). According to the state, the multiplicity of written representations of Mayan languages caused significant damage to the project of transforming monolingual Mayas into literate Spanish-speaking Guatemalans. The IIN reported, "So many difficulties of diverse nature have come to be accentuated when we try to arrive at the literacy of the core indigenous monolingual communities who will have to suffer the transition to a new phonemic system and its consequent representation" (1950:5).[8] Of the forty-seven conference participants addressing this problem, most "experts" were Ladinos and foreign linguists associated with the SIL. Speakers of Mayan languages were generally restricted to the role of "informant," though seven Mayas with professional positions in the IIN also attended. Their discussions centered on the phonetics and phonology of several languages, including Mam, Popti', Chuj, Q'anjob'al, Awakateko, Poqomam, Q'eqchi', Poqomchi', Chorti', K'iche', Kaqchikel, and Tz'utujiil (López 1989:36). Departing from Townsend's earlier emphasis on morphology, discussants called for a vigorous investigation of Mayan languages' sound systems and for ways to represent them in written form. Pivotal in focusing linguistic analysis of Mayan languages on phonetics, the First Linguistics Congress led the way to articulating this focus as an explicitly scientific undertaking.

The proposals instituted by the First Linguistic Congress were codified in the IIN's publication, the *Alfabetos para los cuatro idiomas indígenas mayoritarios de Guatemala: Quiché, cakchiquel, mam y kekchí* (*Alphabets for the Four Major Indigenous Languages of Guatemala*), and they were officialized in a presidential accord in 1950.[9] The orthography and phonetic and phonological analyses presented in this governmental publication are marked by two themes. First, there is a new, explicit invocation of the objective science of linguistics as the legitimating force behind the analysis of languages. Second, there is a recurring iconization of Kaqchikel with Spanish, similar to that seen in earlier linguistic missionary work.

With this publication, then, linguistic analysis took a categorically scientific turn. The change of direction toward "science" co-occurred with the establishment of phonetics as the field's new central object of investigation. Even though substantively redirected, however, linguistics continued to be guided by the same linguistic processes and political agendas that had driven it during its "pre-scientific" days.

The claims of SIL linguists to a scientific enterprise notwithstanding, linguistic analysis at the time did become a more vigorous undertaking than it was earlier in the twentieth century. Unlike earlier linguistic work done by Townsend and other missionary linguists, the technical discourse and textual disciplinary practices of linguistics in this era are fully en-textualized in representations of Kaqchikel phonetics, phonology, and orthography. For example, in *Alfabetos*, pronunciations of sounds are explained vis-à-vis their place and manner of articulation, as in "the /k/ represents the stop of a post-palatal sound" (IIN 1950:14). Also, phonologi-cal rules are written, such as the rule that "the /r/ at the end of the word is retroflexive" (1950:15). Lists of individual sounds are provided in "word initial," "word intermediate," and "word final" position, as in "/m/ *muxu'x* (belly button), *imul* (rabbit) and *imam* (grandchild)" (1950:16).

Taken together, these specific textual models confirm what Bauman and Briggs posit in their theoretical account of language ideologies and modernity, namely, that they "help to concretize the metadiscursive re-gime of linguistics and authorize particular representations of languages, in this case Mayan ones, as legitimate (2003:312). Such descriptive repre-sentations of sounds ostensibly perform a "value-free scientific"—rather than politically situated—analysis of Kaqchikel sounds. In so doing, these representations of Mayan languages grounded in the explicit discourse of science and the textual practices of objective linguistics lend authority to the SIL/IIN's particular orthographic choices. Highlighting the source of their authority, the authors justified their analysis and representation of Kaqchikel sounds in the following way: "This Institute also wants to make clear that we have conformed, wherever possible, to the science of lin-guistics" (1950:10).[10]

It is not fortuitous that the phonetics of Mayan languages (as opposed to other aspects of grammar) became the focus of analysis when linguis-tics took an overtly "scientific" turn. The reasons for this are both political and semiotic. They are political in that regimentation of sound systems can play a central role in the formation of national identity. The regimen-tation of phonetics enables the development of standardized orthogra-phies that, in turn, facilitate the proliferation of textual materials for vernacular literacy as part of national identity formulation. As Schieffelin and Doucet (1994) have illustrated in Haiti, the consolidation of national identities in post-colonial contexts is often predicated upon regimenting sound systems for the production of a unified orthography. A unified orthography, in turn, facilitates textual and social processes by which Benedict Anderson (1991) argues nations are imagined.

In addition to this political explanation, there are also semiotic reasons that may account for the co-occurrence of the scientific turn in linguistics with the particular attention paid to phonetic analysis. The focus of SIL linguists on phonetic analysis provided for them, I argue, a creative index of "expert knowledge" because the phoneme, the smallest meaningful unit within a human language, is taken to be the least likely aspect of a grammatical system accessible to "native speaker" awareness. Renowned SIL linguist Kenneth Pike advances such an epistemological division between "expert analyst" and "native speaker" in his classic text, *Phonemics*:

> The sounds of a language are automatically and unconsciously organized by the native into structural units. . . . One of these sound units may have as submembers numerous slightly different varieties which a trained foreigner might detect but which a native speaker may be unaware of. In fact, if the native is told that such variation exists in the pronunciation of his sound units he may emphatically deny it. (1947:57)

For Pike, trained foreigners are able to detect the nuances of sound patterns within a given language, while native speakers remain unconscious of them. Pike's particular construction of expertise is erected upon a clearly invoked "scientific framing of acoustic and articulatory properties of speech" (Errington 2001:21). In other words, phonetic analysis sustains claims to a scientific enterprise by means of an ostensibly justifiable division between the superior knowledge of the expert linguists and the lack of awareness among native speakers.

SIL missionary linguists are not alone in their focus on the perceived limits of native-speaker awareness. The division between expert knowledge that can accurately penetrate language structure and the relational native's incapacity for reflexive understanding of it is, as Bauman and Briggs argue, deeply rooted in the history of secular linguistic science: "One implication of this principled regimen of discounting is that the scholarly study of language has systematically organized itself around precisely those aspects of linguistic form and practice that are, or are assumed to be, most inaccessible to folk awareness or valid insight" (2000:199).

In particular, attention to meaningful units of sound as comprising a site that is inaccessible to native speakers' awareness is grounded in much contemporary linguistic anthropology inherited, in part, from the pioneering work of Franz Boas. Boas articulated such a position in his foundational *Introduction to Handbook of American Indian Languages*: "A single sound as such has no independent existence, it never enters into the consciousness of the speaker. . . . Phonetic elements become conscious to us only as a result of analysis" (1966:19–20). From this canonical perspective, it is only through the linguist's trained attention that the grammatical subtleties of distinctive sounds can be perceived.

While Boas established such an orientation toward the analysis of sound, it has also been further developed in contemporary linguistic anthropology. Michael Silverstein, in his foundational essay "Limits of Awareness" (1981), develops a theoretical model to account for the level of accuracy in native speakers' linguistic consciousness based upon semiotic principles. "It is extremely difficult, if not impossible, to make a native speaker take account of those readily discernible facts of speech as action that (s)he has no ability to describe for us in his or her own language" (1981:3). Building upon Whorf's work, Silverstein argues that the degree to which native speakers are able to accurately articulate metalinguistic (specifically metapragmatic) knowledge of their language(s) depends upon three semiotic properties: unavoidable referentiality, continuous segmentability, and relative presuppositional quality vis-à-vis the context of usage (1981:5). With all three properties, Silverstein finds in the sounds of human speech the exception that proves the rule of native speakers' limited awareness. For instance, he contrasts the T/V deference versus the solidarity system, which is unavoidably referential, with

> such pragmatic alternations as certain North American English phonetic markers of social stratification isolated by Labov in many famous studies, where the signals of socio-economic class affiliation of the speaker reside in subtle pronunciation effects within certain phonetic categories, which operate independent of any segmentation of speech by the criterion of reference. (1981:5)

Similarly, he contrasts continuous segmentability with the augmentative-neutral-diminutive form changes in Wasco-Wishram in order to exemplify another aspect of sound systems beyond native speaker awareness:

"In isolating the signals of the alternation, we are isolating not segments of speech, but phonological features of some of the segments; we are not isolating thereby any units of language that themselves have referential value" (1981:9). Finally, Silverstein concludes his discussion about the limits of native speaker awareness by contrasting surface lexical forms with sounds and other nonsegmentable aspects of language structure: "The further we get from these kinds of functional elements of language, the less we can guarantee awareness on the part of the native speakers. . . . Hence for the rest, the more we have to depend upon cross-cultural analysis and the accumulated technical insight" (1981:20). Silverstein's logic underscores the perspective that, since sound cannot be segmented, it can be accurately understood only by the technical expertise of language analysts. This perspective implies a relational and deep epistemological division between expert analysts and common native speakers.

Following eminent linguistic anthropologists before him, then, Silverstein extends the conventional line of thinking, according to which sound enables a line to be drawn between technical "expert" knowledge and lay-speaker understanding. To the degree that we recognize this division, and look to sound and sound systems as inaccessible to the "common knowledge" of native speakers, we must also consider my argument that "expert" linguistic knowledge belongs to those who can produce metalinguistic discourse about sounds and sound systems—namely, the linguist trained in systematic descriptive phonetic analysis. Thus, this particular epistemological distinction functions in the manner that Bauman and Briggs identify in their historical analysis of language ideologies and inequality. It authorizes the linguist as "legislator on the basis of claims to superior knowledge to make authoritative statements about the maintenance and perfection of the social order in the service of state power" (2003:308–9).

The Proyecto Lingüístico Francisco Marroquín: Good Science and the Politics of Difference

While the SIL and IIN linguists' scientific analyses of Kaqchikel sounds worked in service of state power to assimilate speakers of Mayan languages to Spanish, as we will see below, the role of the linguist as a modern "legislator" can indeed also function to *challenge* state power. In the early to mid-twentieth century, the SIL dominated linguistic analysis of Mayan languages, in part through the support it received by the Guatemalan state. Beginning in the mid-1970s, professional Mayas were more systematic in their challenge of SIL's authority to research, analyze, and represent Mayan languages with the support of secular North American linguists in service of cultural rights activism. Not surprisingly, their challenge to the authority of the SIL engendered concomitant struggles over phonetic analyses and orthographic representations.

In 1972, secular North Americans formed the Proyecto Lingüístico Francisco Marroquín (PLFM), a nongovernmental organization (NGO) dedicated to the linguistic analysis of Mayan languages in Guatemala. Senior cultural anthropologist Kay Warren recalls its early history:

> Bob Gersony, a driven self-educated Vietnam vet; Jo Froman, a Midwestern philosophy B.A. studying Kaqchikel as part of her Peace Corp training; Tony Jackson, an Oxford-trained British volunteer; and Terry Kaufman, a well-known American research linguist—took over the center from a pair of tired American priests, who had run a language program for missionaries and used Mayas as passive informants for their studies. Soon thereafter three rounds of Peace Corps volunteers with M.A. or Ph.D. degrees in linguistics joined the rejuvenated project as instructors—this time to offer professional training to Mayas. (1998:x)

From the hands of Catholic priests to the leadership of "progressive" North Americans (Warren 1998), the early years of the Proyecto Lingüístico Francisco Marroquín (PLFM) were marked by the involvement of several North American secular linguists, including Terrence Kaufman, Nora England, Judith Maxwell, Laura Martin, and Karen Dakin, who trained Mayas in linguistic analysis and who have become senior scholars in the field.[11] These scholars conducted linguistic research under the auspices of the PLFM until state-sponsored violence escalated at the end of the decade. In 1975, the PLFM made a monumental step toward the goal of Maya linguistic self-determination. It became legally, professionally, and administratively Maya—the first autonomous Maya NGO dedicated to linguistic analysis.[12]

Like the SIL, with its stated commitment to the scientific analysis of Mayan languages, the PLFM centered its mission on the development of scientific linguistic research. Unlike the SIL, the PLFM also underscored

—as it does to date—a linguistic science both *by Mayas* and *for Mayas*, a goal that directly challenged the inherited model of expert knowledge by undermining the division between expert analysts and native speakers. This challenge was immediately apparent in the stated objectives of the PLFM, which included

> to be a center of technical resources in linguistics, made up of native speakers of different Mayan languages, properly chosen and trained; and to provide intensive and technical training for native speakers of Mayan languages with respect to the development of linguistic and educational expertise, with the goal to promote the languages, endowing them with dictionaries, syntactic structure, and cultural diffusion. (López 1989:53–54)[13]

Explicit in the PLFM's mission was a strong interrelation of expert knowledge, scientific analysis, and Maya professionalization in the field, in which the analysts are native speakers of Mayan languages and the speakers acquire the technical expertise to become analysts, thereby blurring the tacit division between them inherited from linguistic science.

This comprised a strikingly different epistemology from that construed by the SIL, which had defined the subject of expert linguistic knowledge tautologically, as the scientific linguist/analyst. Still configured around the goal of scientific analysis, the legislator of expert knowledge erected by PLFM was the native speaker of Mayan languages—a member of the Maya ethnolinguistic community—who would undergo a process of professionalization that depended on rather than denied the linguistic and cultural identity of the would-be scientific analyst. This new epistemological reconfiguration provided a distinct manner of linking linguistics and politics; it situated scientific linguistic analysis as a tool for challenging the non-Indian hegemony that excluded Mayas and their languages from the national imaginary. This orientation is best captured in the following directive of Maya anthropologist, Margarita López Raquec:

> We need to define and apply a linguistic politics oriented to the promotion of Mayan languages, not as an isolated factor, but rather as a component that gives identity, strength, and continuity to the Maya people. The [linguistic] information contributes to the process of self-determination and, specifically when compared to the path of preserving Mayan languages, the majority of Mayan speakers lack the information necessary

to take part in the decisions. In this way, [the linguistic information] will contribute to those directly responsible for Mayan languages, Mayas themselves, so that they may have the necessarily elements to make use of linguistic rights (López 1989:9–11).[14]

Guided by an explicit political vision of Maya linguistic rights and cultural autonomy, PLFM linguists developed a new orthography for Mayan languages in 1976 that would consolidate Mayan linguistic struggles for self-determination around linguistic difference.[15] Along with a scientific method informing their written representation of Mayan languages' sounds, the PLFM also posited orthographic choices based upon "rational" principles, many of which had already been developed by North American secular PLFM linguist Terrence Kaufman for the general purpose of creating orthographies for Native American languages. Invoking this explicitly modernist principle of rationality, PLFM linguists argued against adopting a strictly Spanish writing system to represent Mayan languages because they regarded it as fundamentally marred by several "irrational" aspects. They showed, for instance, that the phoneme /k/ was irrationally represented in the Spanish alphabet by several characters, including *c*, *qu*, and *k* (López 1989:58).

While invoking rationality as guiding force in its work, the PLFM further elaborated its criteria for developing alphabets: (1) all letters and combinations of letters that indicate a single phoneme must be pronounced, (2) each phoneme should have its corresponding written form (letter or combination of letters), and (3) each phoneme should be written in one way and not in various ways (López 1989:56).[16] Through these criteria, the PLFM sought to establish an isomorphic relationship between an individual sound (phoneme) and its written representation (grapheme). Furthermore, they posited this seemingly transparent relationship as sound linguistic analysis based solely on rational principles. Successful in perfecting the earlier attempts by Maya professionals such as Chávez to establish the essential linguistic difference of Mayan languages through iconization, the PLFM's efforts illustrated, as Irvine and Gal put it, how "the iconicity of the ideological representation reinforces the implication of necessity" (2000:37–38). In effect, the PLFM created a process for attaining a regimentation of the sound systems of Mayan languages, which would establish linguistic difference on a scientific and rational basis, and which would pave the way for making assertions of cultural difference by native speakers/analysts. Such assertions of cultural difference, in turn, provide the basis upon which a unified people, in this case the Pueblo Maya, have made some limited, yet successful, political claims for self-representation upon the Guatemalan nation, such as the rights recognized in the Ley de Idiomas Nacionales.

Applied Linguistics and the Politics of Assimilation

The success of the PLFM's claims to scientific expertise became evident as early as the late seventies, when SIL/IIN linguists, shifting from their earlier position, began to challenge "scientific" linguistics from the perspective of "applied" linguistics. This rhetorical and analytic change from an "objective" to a "practical" orientation toward linguistic analysis can be seen as an effort to bolster the SIL's own waning authority regarding their phonetic analyses and orthographies that functioned in service of Spanish linguistic assimilation. In 1977, SIL linguists published *Alfabetos de las lenguas mayances (The Mayan Languages Alphabets)* through the San Carlos National University.[17] In it, the authors made explicit their particular political orientation and posited, as the ultimate end of their linguistic analyses, the transformation of monolingual Mayas into literate Spanish speakers and readers. Their political goals were in explicit accordance with the stated goals of the National Bilingual Education Program, with which they collaborated (Cojtí 1990). Reversing its earlier claims to conduct scientific analyses of Mayan languages, the SIL shifted its orientation to a more "practical" one that would best facilitate the dissemination of Spanish literacy among Maya peoples. SIL linguists claimed to "work exclusively in applied linguistics for teaching, or rather, without pretending to symbolize subtleties of pronunciation that would only be of interest to rigorously scientific investigation" (IIN 1977:11).[18]

Eschewing the utility of detailed scientific investigation in the SIL's new position, Marilyn Henne, associate director for academic programs in the SIL's Central American branch, criticized Maya linguists' phonetic analyses and graphemic choices as impractical because they were contrary to "instrumental use of the alphabets for preparing materials necessary to the bilingual education program" (1991:4). Furthermore, Henne remarked, despite new and increasing Maya scholarly expertise in linguistics, Maya linguists' attention to pressing matters like "practical decoding and pedagogical issues appears irrelevant" (1991:5). Henne's critique charges that Maya concerns with "scientific" linguistics are merely esoteric and symbolic, while the concerns of SIL linguists are more relevant because they are directed toward creating literate, Spanish-speaking Mayas that will advance national progress and integration in Guatemala.

The Mayan Languages Academy of Guatemala and Linguistic Self-Determination

In 1984, as state-sponsored violence against Maya communities began to subside in rural areas, the Segundo Congreso Lingüístico Nacional (Second National Linguistic Congress) convened in the city of Quetzaltenango.[19] Military personnel joined Maya linguists, North American missionary linguists, North American secular linguists, and elite Ladino scholars to address the effects of multilingualism in Guatemala and to debate language planning.[20] Several recommendations were made at the conclusion of the four-day conference, the most significant of which for Mayan linguistics and consolidating ethnolinguistic identity was the recommendation to create a new institution that would deal exclusively with the analysis and promotion of Mayan languages in Guatemala. The recommendation called for "the creation of a Mayan Languages Academy made up of linguists, especially speakers of Mayan languages" (Ministerio de Educación 1985:147). The proposal underscored the importance of "native" speaker participation, defined in ethnolinguistic terms, and expertise in indigenous linguistic analysis.[21]

The first official responsibility of the Academia de Lenguas Mayas de Guatemala (ALMG) as an autonomous Maya institution was "to study in detail linguistic, pedagogical and other aspects of the proposed alphabets for each language" (Ministerio de Educación 1985:147), a responsibility that signaled the political urgency of regimenting Mayan languages' sounds into an authoritative graphemic representation.[22] ALMG representatives undertook this charge amidst a great deal of linguistic, ethnic, religious, "practical," and political strife.[23] In June of 1987, the recently constituted ALMG organized a meeting held at the Centro de Investigaciones Regionales de Mesoamérica (CIRMA). Nora England recalls the momentous event: "Almost a hundred Maya met in 1987, established criteria for the selection of alphabets for their languages, listened to opinions of non-Maya experts who attended the meeting . . . and voted on the selection of a common alphabet" (1996:183). The new Unified Alphabet for Mayan languages voted upon at the meeting was strikingly similar to the earlier alphabet, with the exception of one grapheme, crafted by Kaufman and the PLFM in 1976. The exclusively Maya group did make one change: the apostrophe (') instead of the 7 was chosen to represent the glottal stop, perhaps a minor concession to SIL/IIN linguists who regularly used the apostrophe for that grapheme.[24] The creation of the new ALMG and its Unified Alphabet underscore the union of scientific analysis with a politics of cultural autonomy for Maya ethnolinguistic groups. Put another way, this shift in authoritative Mayan linguistics demonstrates the continued importance of scientifically based representations of sounds (and their regimentation in written form) by Maya experts to further counterhegemonic efforts for inclusion at the national level.

With the creation of the ALMG and its alphabetic victory, there was a shift in the struggle between SIL/IIN linguists and Maya linguists over who would be recognized as legitimate experts on Mayan languages and who would produce the most authoritative linguistic, particularly phonetic, analyses and orthographic representations. It was a monumental shift in twentieth-century Guatemalan Mayan linguistics in both experts and politics that was ridiculed by some and embraced by others. While secular North American scholars supported the emergent Maya leadership in the study of Mayan languages for the political end of self-determination, SIL linguists contested this new direction. Shortly after the historic meeting at CIRMA, SIL linguists began a campaign to discredit the new alphabet and its authors' political project among local Maya communities. "Their tactics included promoting letter- and petition-writing campaigns supposedly initiated by rural Maya . . . to broadcasting a number of radio advertisements against the alphabets which said, among other things, that now people's Maya last names would be misspelled and mispronounced, and ultimately to making a 'human rights' complaint about the alphabet" (England 1996:184). On the cultural front, the possibility of a spelling change in Maya names was linked to the possibility of injustice on the economic front. Judith Maxwell recalled that SIL linguists and evangelical Maya workers supported a popular rumor that

Maya people would lose title to their lands because many Maya have indigenous last names spelled with a Spanish-like orthography. If the new orthography went into place, they would jeopardize their legal standing as owners because the spelling of their names would change (personal communication, 2003). The legacy of SIL opposition to the Unified Alphabet and Maya linguistic self-determination has remained visible into the late twentieth century, even as the SIL presence in Guatemala has diminished substantially.[25] Nora England explains the ideological legacy of SIL analyses and politics: "One of the principal negative effects of the SIL campaign against the new alphabet was that it promoted the basic idea that it is essentially difficult to read in a Mayan language and that any change (even if relatively minor) would make it impossible" (1996:184).

While Evangelical linguists challenged Maya linguists' authority, North American secular linguists and scholars who had led the field of Mayan linguistics in earlier decades became consultants to Maya scholars. The new advisory role in Mayan linguistics was performed during the historical alphabet debates, when North American linguists offered their professional opinions but were excluded from the final vote (England 1996:183). These scholars actively espouse and continue to promote the project of Maya autonomy and cultural self-determination (England 1996; Maxwell 1996; Schele and Grube 1996) within the Guatemalan nation-state.

Maya linguists and scholars look to the official recognition of the Unified Alphabet and the subsequent officialization of the ALMG in 1990 as substantial victories in their struggle for linguistic self-representation and cultural self-determination. This perspective informs the Maya scholars' self-conscious position that the Guatemalan nation must be fundamentally reconceptualized as multilingual and multicultural. For example, the linguists of Oxlajuuj Keej Maya' Ajtz'iib' (OKMA) explained the significance of their grammatical research in the following way:

> Knowledge of the social, linguistic, and cultural reality of the Guatemalan state is a must for all of its inhabitants. . . . Guatemala is a multicultural and multilingual country, a reality that is unknown or rejected by many people. The Maya nation, that forms the majority of the population of the country, possesses its own values that constitute a great human richness. Among those strongest values that are found are the twenty Mayan languages spoken today. (1993:1)

Such scholarly and political interventions by Maya linguists underscore the possibility of making efficacious claims on the nation to cultural rights based upon a strategically essential linguistic difference that unifies its speakers as an ethnolinguistic group. These accomplishments of Maya linguists are doubly significant because they demonstrate how Maya activists and scholars have managed to challenge the modernist project of nation-building based upon ideals of cultural continuity and ethnic homogeneity (Handler 1988) in that they have obliged the Guatemalan state to shift its position on the relation of difference within the nation from the antithetical to the problematic (French 2008:112).

Since the development of the ALMG, Maya scholars have continued to use linguistic analyses and print technologies to bring their vision of a new multiethnic, multicultural, and multilingual Guatemalan nation into being, as I outlined in chapter 1. Raxche Demetrio Rodríguez Guaján explicitly articulated the ideological connection between a new multicultural Guatemalan national community and democratic social principles in the introduction to *Rukemik K'ak'a' Taq Tzij*:

> Mayan languages are testimonies of the will to be and to continue being a nation by the Mayas of today. The languages have been maintained relatively strongly despite that their speakers have not been prepared with vigorous educational programs that favor their cultural and linguistic development until the present moment. Nevertheless, the new times that Guatemala is beginning to live, particularly in the formulation of the right that Mayas receive an education in their own language, necessitates many activities . . . that make this legitimate right viable. These rights will particularly benefit new generations of Guatemalan Mayas. (Kaqchikel Cholchi' 1995:7)[26]

With the creation of the ALMG, the struggle of Maya linguists to become recognized legitimate agents in a state-sponsored institution is nearly over. The proposal to create an autonomous governmental agency dedicated to Mayan languages was part of a thread that for several decades continued to unfold in response to a persistently perceived need for expert linguists and scientific linguistic analyses. Throughout this continuous thread, which extended alongside the development and consolidation of a scientific perspective on linguistics in Guatemala, there are several reasons why one may wish to question the perceived status of linguistics as a science, or to scrutinize the various claims made to lend authority to this status.

Nevertheless, it was by upholding the scientific paradigm of linguistics that Mayan analysts were able to change the direction of linguistics for explicitly political ends. While it may be true that Mayan linguists, as much as their SIL/IIN counterparts, misrecognized the science of linguistics as the legitimate epistemology for regimenting Mayan languages, it is also true that such a misrecognition was key to their successful efforts in guiding linguistics away from the once-dominant, state-sponsored practices directed at eradicating cultural and linguistic difference and aimed at forming the Guatemalan nation around an exclusive and homogeneous vision. Thus, scientific epistemology, what Bauman and Briggs identify as "the wellspring of modernity" (2003:4), is used strategically to challenge the explicitly homogenizing and exclusionary goals of what Anderson calls the "most universally legitimate political form" of modern times (1991). Nevertheless, it is a struggle that continues to unfold in the face of national and international homogenizing projects that allow "cultural difference" only in circumscribed ways (Hale 2006).

While Maya scholars have used linguistic science for counterhegemonic purposes to challenge their exclusion from the Guatemalan nation, their efforts also confirm what Bauman and Briggs suggest in their conclusion to the historical study of language ideologies, modernist discourse, and inequality. Bauman and Briggs posit that "contemporary critical projects themselves bolster key foundations of the modernity that they claim to challenge," thereby furthering inequality in unintended ways (2003:309). Indeed, as the Pan-Maya movement produces new indigenous experts to regiment language and culture, it contributes to the creation of what Bauman and Briggs call the "power/knowledge syndrome" in which the intellectual, as "legislator," is authorized on the basis of claims to superior knowledge to make authoritative statements about the "maintenance and perfection of the social order" (2003:309). In this case, the creation of an essentialized notion of Maya ethnolinguistic identity excludes those indigenous people who do not or cannot define Maya identity in ethnolinguistic terms. However, as we will see in subsequent chapters, Maya linguists' project of linguistic unification around Maya ethnolinguistic identity is challenged by locally held and experienced ideologies of linguistic tradition. In other words, local constructions of language and tradition challenge the tacit gestures of exclusion that the critical Pan-Maya project unwittingly reinscribes.

CHAPTER 3

Traditional Histories, Local Selves, and Challenges to Linguistic Unification

The Standardization of Mayan Languages

Max Weinreich's famous adage that "a language is a dialect with an army" underscores the role of power in defining some linguistic varieties and not others as legitimate and authentic languages.[1] He may have put it better were he to have said, "A language is a dialect with an army *of linguists.*" Indeed, the last day of the linguistics sessions at the Third Congress of Maya Studies held in August of 2001 was rife with struggle and strategy among scholars of language. As I mentioned in the preface, this biannual conference first convened in 1996 as part of an opening in public discourse during the peace accords era. As such, its participants were actively engaged with the Guatemalan state's new commitment to recognize and support Maya cultural difference. The structures, statuses, and uses of Mayan languages figured centrally in this recently articulated project of reconceptualizing the Guatemalan nation as more inclusive in ethnolinguistc terms. With keen attention to cultural and linguistic politics at the national level, the Congress of Maya Studies became a key foundation in what Bauman and Briggs (2003) call the establishment of an institutional infrastructure for "expert" tasks that create new forms of authority and hierarchy (308). This creation of intellectual and institutional infrastructure for experts is one of the "most conspicuous attributes of modernity" that Bauman and Briggs argue merits careful scrutiny by anthropologists concerned with language ideologies and inequality (308). Therefore, we can look to debates at the Maya Studies Congress as key sites for investigation because new forms of authority and hierarchy may be created by experts even as they seek further inclusion for Maya people at the national level.

In fact, the Third Congress drew young Maya university students, senior Maya academics who had lived through the Violence, U.S. secular linguists and anthropologists (including me), European scholars, and a few missionary linguists from the Summer Institute of Linguistics (SIL). These experts-in-training and established experts addressed a broad range of linguistic topics, such as particles in seventeenth-century Kaqchikel, passive voice in nominal syntagms, grammaticalization in Popti', criteria for the separation of morphemes in Mam, and the influence of Mayan languages on Spanish in Guatemala. When the last panel of the Third Congress, "Experiences with Standardization," convened, it came as no surprise that the audience grew to standing room only given the centrality of standardization to the Pan-Maya ethnolinguistic project and its inter-locutors. I, like many others who attended the conference, had spent the morning listening to jokes about the representatives and speculations about the outcome of anticipated events. Jovial informal talk was inter-mingled with an intense concern about what position the Academia de Lenguas Mayas de Guatemala (ALMG) would take on the question of Mayan languages standardization efforts. In particular, most conference participants were focused on the very polemic process of selecting par-ticular local varieties of each Mayan language to codify.

As each male panelist from exclusively Maya institutions—including the ALMG, Oxlajuuj Keej Maya' Ajtz'iib' (OKMA), Kaqchikel Cholchi', and the Guatemalan Center for Bilingual and Intercultural Education (DIJEBI)—carefully articulated his vision for linguistic unification, it be-came immediately evident that the positions taken among experts were deeply conflicting. The ALMG panelist, for instance, argued that "the main priority in moving ahead with linguistic standardization is to take into full account the views of the local speakers," while a panelist from OKMA claimed that "decisions about language standardization should not be in the hands of the entire speech community because standardiza-tion is not a popular decision. It is a technical one."

The tensions between popular and technical understandings of Ma-yan languages have emerged out of the recent transformation of linguis-tics as an authoritative science linked to various national political proj-ects. As I outlined in the previous chapter, linguistic analysis in the early twentieth century done by the SIL functioned hegemonically in service of state interests to assimilate Mayas into Spanish-speaking Guatemalans.

Linguistics directed by Mayas for Mayas at the end of the twentieth century was an explicitly counterhegemonic endeavor to create a more multicultural, democratic, and inclusive nation. In this unprecedented historical moment, when native speakers are expert analysts and expert analysts are native speakers, there seems to be only one point of consensus among them: "Maya all agree that Maya should do the choosing in the process of standardization" (England 1996:182). Beyond that, as the division among panelists about language standardization indicates, there is much contestation. Local versus ethnolinguistic definitions of Maya identity are at the center of these struggles.

The question of which language varieties should be codified as standards is highly debated among expert speakers/analysts and the various local indigenous communities from which they come. The terms of debate among Maya communities are often centered on distinct epistemological claims to local historical tradition and to modern linguistic science as the legitimate basis for decision making. Given that most Mayan languages do not have an agreed-upon prestige dialect (England 1996:182), it is not surprising that Maya peoples tend to articulate a great loyalty to and preference for the language variety spoken in their local community. This local dialect preference corresponds to commonplace definitions of indigenous identity as grounded in individual geographic communities (Tax 1937; Bunzel 1959; Warren 1978; Watanabe 1992; Richards 1998; Reynolds 2002) rather than in ethnolinguistic ones. Because almost all twenty Mayan languages are highly diverse in terms of dialect differentiation and subdialect local variation (England 1996:182),[2] the ideology of community language loyalty reinscribes local over Pan-Maya understandings of indigenous identity and privileges dialect heterogeneity over the linguistic homogeneity inherent in standardization projects like the ones currently developing for Mayan languages in Guatemala.

Maya activists and scholars tend to view Maya communities' preference for local varieties as exacerbating the fragmentation of Mayan languages and peoples, a process they see as a direct consequence of Spanish colonialism (Maxwell 1996). They argue that the colonial administrative units developed by the Spaniards, still functioning in the contemporary political administrative configuration of the Guatemalan nation-state, fragmented preexisting indigenous ethnolinguistic borders (see fig. 1). For this reason, Maya linguists are generally opposed to analyses that

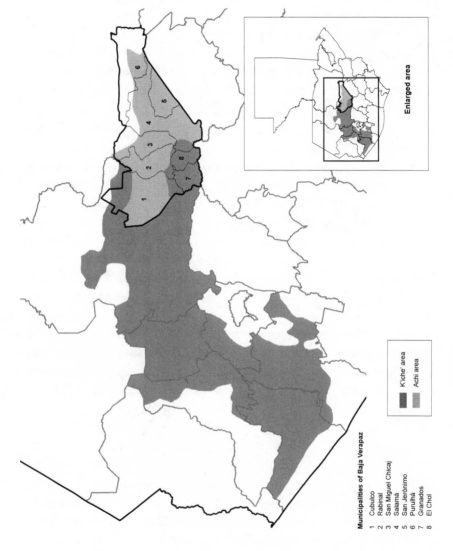

Municipalities of Baja Verapaz

1 Cubulco
2 Rabinal
3 San Miguel Chicaj
4 Salamá
5 San Jerónimo
6 Purulhá
7 Granados
8 El Chol

K'iche' area
Achi area

Enlarged area

Figure 3. K'iche' and Achi ethnolinguistic communities (by Kathryn Dunn).

highlight local dialect difference, seeing them as merely enhancing linguistic fragmentation and as seriously undermining the project of Mayan languages standardization and concomitant political unification around ethnolinguistic identification. Standardization is politically urgent in the case of Maya ethnonationalism precisely because it has the possibility to be a productive act of linguistic consolidation that can be recursively projected onto collective identity consolidation (Irvine and Gal 2000)—a unified linguistic code begins to stand for a culturally unified people. However, the efficacy of native linguists to regiment language varieties through modern linguistic science is challenged by locally held ideologies of language, sometimes in linguists' own natal communities. This contestation complicates Bauman and Briggs's theoretical account of expert knowledge in that it demonstrates that "expert" authority is not easily or universally recognized as legitimate. Such challenges to expert knowledge become particularly visible in an ongoing public debate over a language variety known as Achi. At issue in this debate is the definition of Achi as a language or dialect. Figure 3 illustrates the ethnolinguistically defined borders of Achi and K'iche' varieties. At stake in this map and the debate it represents is the struggle between the epistemologies of modern linguistic science and local historical tradition. These conflicting epistemologies are central to competing notions of collective indigenous identity that each side engenders. As we will see, local understandings of history problematize Pan-Maya homogenization efforts. In so doing, local ideologies of linguistic tradition resist expert representations of language and identity that privilege unity at the ethnolinguistic level.

K'iche'/Achi Ethnolinguistic Group(s)?

Achi is spoken by approximately fifteen thousand people who live in the Baja Verapaz department communities of Rabinal, San Miguel Chicaj, San Jeronimo, Salamá, and Cubulco (Sis Iboy 2002). Terrence Kaufman, "grandfather" of modern Mayan linguistics, argued in no uncertain terms in *Idiomas de Mesoamérica* (1974) that Achi is a dialect of K'iche', the Mayan language most widely spoken in Guatemala. Nevertheless, local ideologies in the area rely on historical tradition to define Achi as an autonomous language quite distinct from K'iche'. Both Maya and North American scholars agree that the name of the variety, Achi—meaning "man" in both Achi and K'iche'—is most likely derived from the name of the *Rabinal Achi* (Sis Iboy 2002; Tedlock 2003), a pre-Columbian oral drama from the Rabinal community preserved in writing and one of very few indigenous texts to survive the Spanish invasion of the 1500s. After various waves of suppression by outsiders during the past five centuries, the *Rabinal Achi*, as Dennis Tedlock explains, is an exemplar of traditional expressive culture that was still performed at the beginning of the twenty-first century (2003).[3]

A brief look at the *Rabinal Achi* drama suffices to demonstrate the lasting effects that this traditional text has had on the community. The play and its contemporarily performed instantiations inform local positions on the status of Achi as an autonomous language, a language clearly named and demarcated from the K'iche' language and the K'iche' people. The central concern of the tale is the pre-Columbian invasion of the Rabinal community by a former K'iche' ally. Kaweq, historical leader of the K'iche', is captured and eventually sacrificed by Rabinal Achi (the Man from Rabinal). Before he is put to death, Kaweq reveals that he has secretly cursed the land of Rabinal. With every contemporary performance of the play, members of the Rabinal community are reminded of Kaweq's curse, as well as of the invasion by the K'iche's. More than a mere reminder of events in the remote past, the play enacts what, within Maya notions of time, is seen as force in the present. The contemporary enactment of a past drama, then, shows more than a people's effort to give current significance to their history; it shows how a given people "use the meanings of the past to organize the present while deploying present meanings to organize the past" (Kelleher 2003:21). Therefore, for many Achi speakers, the play enacts dramatically a historical experience that informs local ideology, namely that many members of the local Rabinal-Maya community consider the K'iche's their enemies and often refer to them as such (Sis Iboy 2002). Thus, the border between historically separate political communities during pre-Columbian times (Sis Iboy 2002; Tedlock 2003) is recursively projected onto perceived contemporary linguistic separation. As a result, Achi speakers see differences in linguistic form with K'iche' speakers to be continuous with historically prior and culturally deeper divisions. In other words, from the perspective of indigenous people in Rabinal and surrounding environs, the distinction between Achi and K'iche' is firmly grounded in local "tradition." This local tradition is frequently animated when individuals organically refer to themselves in discourse as Achi. For example, Dominga Sic Ruiz, survivor of the Río Negro, Rabinal, massacre during the Violence, reflected on her life as an orphaned victim of genocide: "I wish I could just be a normal Achi woman, but I can't" (Flynn 2002).

Secular North American linguists, and the Maya linguists whom they have trained, seriously call into question the validity of recognizing Achi as an independent language. The criterion for making these determinations, they argue, ought to be linguistic science, not historical tradition. Dennis Tedlock captures the perspective of scientifically trained secular linguists, North American and Maya, with the following remarks: "In terms of linguistics as practiced in the academy, the case for a separate language is weak. People from Rabinal and people who speak even the most distant of K'iche' dialects have little difficulty in conversing with one another" (2003:5). Nora England advances this scholarly understanding:

> This variety [Achi] is clearly a dialect of K'ichee' rather than a separate language. In linguistic terms, it is no more divergent from other dialects of K'ichee' than they are from each other, and its time of separation from other dialects of K'ichee' (using standard lexico-statistic methodology) is relatively short, far short of the time that is usually necessary to establish separate languages. (1996:192)

This disciplinary linguistic ideology that privileges the referential function of language (ignoring pragmatic functions) has been the cornerstone of much decontextualized linguistic analysis that is taken to be value free (Silverstein 1976; Bauman and Briggs 2003). The referential transparency between K'iche' and Achi functions to confirm the scientific epistemology that posits that they are indeed a single language. However, this scientific epistemology was subverted in 1990 when the Guatemalan Mayan Languages Academy recognized Achi as a distinct Mayan language. This recognition privileged local knowledge grounded in the tradition of the Rabinal community over the expert knowledge of linguists based upon modernist epistemologies.[4] In this way, the elevation of tradition over science complicates Bauman and Briggs's theoretical account in that it shows how "tradition" does not consistently lend itself to the articulation of social exclusions that are created by expert analysts (2003:11). Instead, it shows how "tradition" may be used to bolster claims against incipient social exclusions that experts create, such as the exclusion of local definitions of identity.

The ongoing Achi debate demonstrates the contestation between two distinct epistemologies mobilized by indigenous language speakers in highland Guatemala. On the one hand, the scientific epistemology of modern linguistics is strategically used to engender linguistic homogeneity through the erasure of dialect variation. On the other, traditional ways of knowing underscore the multiplicity of language varieties linked with local communities. The former works in service of crafting a collective Maya ethnolinguistic identity, while the latter functions to recreate community-specific definitions of indigenous identity that are particularly strong at the grassroots level among most highland Maya communities in Guatemala (Bunzel 1959; Richards 1998; Watanabe 1992; England 1996; Reynolds 2002). What further complicates the Achi debate are the recent efforts it has generated among native linguists to mediate these two seemingly mutually exclusive epistemologies—science and tradition—and to orchestrate two antithetical pulls—toward Maya ethnolinguistic unification and toward local difference—in a similar direction.

One concrete site of these efforts lies in the research and analyses done by Nikte' Maria Juliana Sis Iboy, who comes from the Rabinal *municipio* with the support of her colleagues at OKMA. In order to appreciate the ways in which Nikte's work mediates the epistemologies of linguistic science and historical tradition, it is important to consider briefly her experiences with indigenous identity, formal education, and scholarly analysis. Like Don Fidencio, whose experiences I discussed in the first chapter, Nikte' grew up in a predominately Maya monolingual household in a rural area. However, Nikte's first language was Achi (instead of Kaqchikel). As we will see, Nikte's early life as a child growing up during the violence of the 1970s resonates with Don Fidencio's narratives of imposed Spanish instruction for the purpose of national cultural assimilation to "non-Indian" ways. As a young monolingual Achi speaker, Nikte' began to learn Spanish at the age of eight when she first entered a public school and was taught by a Spanish-monolingual Ladino. In an informal interview with me, Nikte' recalled the alienation she felt in the classroom:

1) Yo (1), cuando empecé a estudiar, y::, yo tenía ocho años, cuando
   I, when I began to study, and, I was eight years old, when
2) empecé a ir a la escuela. Y no sabía hablar nada, nada en
   I began to go to school. And I didn't know how to speak any, any
3) castellano, ni una palabra, nada. Entonces, fui a la escuela y
   Spanish, not even one word, nothing. So, I went to school and
4) no entendía nada de lo que decía el profesor, era un hombre,
   I didn't understand anything that the professor said, he was a man,
5) no entendía nada. Y pero fui. Y el, pero el primero
   I didn't understand anything. But I went. And the, but the first
6) año era de castellanización.
   year was dedicated to basic Spanish literacy and speaking.

In the first year of her formal education, Nikte' attended an intensive, mandatory Spanish literacy class meant to teach indigenous children Spanish *por pura fuerza* ("by the sheer force") of an exclusively monolingual education in a foreign language. When Nikte' completed third grade, there were no further educational opportunities available for children in her impoverished community. With the support of her parents, she decided to complete elementary school in the more urban environs of neighboring Salamá in a school with few indigenous students, many Ladino children, and exclusively Spanish instruction. After earning an elementary-level education, Nikte' continued to persist in seeking further opportunities to study by traveling even further from her family to the Sololá department in a predominantly Kaqchikel-speaking area. There, she lived in residence and eventually graduated from high school. In the struggle for a basic high-school-level education, Nikte' was forced to leave her family at great financial and emotional cost to them. Nikte's experience as a young indigenous girl desperately seeking education in a structurally racist society provides a telling example of one way that Rigoberta Menchú's (1983) testimony accurately represents the harsh daily realities of many Maya people's lives in Guatemala. Reflecting on the arduous process of formal education in a Ladino-dominated institution, Nikte' focused on the powerful and often destructive forces of state education for indigenous peoples in Guatemala.

7) Cuando la persona ha estudiado, bueno, la educación formal es,
   When a person has studied, well, the formal education is,

8) es (1), horrible porque es un, porque el sistema educativo, es,
   is, horrible because it is, because the educational system is
9) es, no está nada, nada, nada de acuerdo con la cultura
   is, it is not in any, any, any, way in accordance with Maya
10) maya. Entonces, más, más, en vez de, de, hacer más persona, a
    culture. So, more, more, instead of making more a person,
11) la persona, y, y digamos educarles dentro de su cultura
    of the person, and, and, let's say, educate them within their culture
12) lo aleja, lo saca de su cultura y la meten otra.
    they distance him, they remove him from his culture and they put in another.

Like many other Maya people who struggled for the opportunity to study, Nikte' experienced formal education as a powerful agent of Ladino hegemony that removed one's culture and inserted another both literally and metaphorically (line 12). Nikte' was physically distanced from her family and conceptually distanced from her values and identity as an indigenous girl by entering a Ladino-dominated educational system. From Nikte's perspective, the embodied and objectified foreign culture is perceived to be in direct conflict with her own Maya culture (lines 9–10).

In this oppressive context, Nikte' came to study a more "libratory" linguistic science. In 1989, Nikte' received intensive training in descriptive linguistics in a course designed exclusively for Mayas, taught by Nora England in a Guatemalan urban center. Nikte' was selected as an outstanding student and continued to study with Professor England. Soon after, she enrolled in an advanced-degree linguistics program at the private Rafael Landívar University (URL) in Guatemala. Nikte' is among the first generation of Maya women in Guatemala ever to complete an advanced university degree. As such, Nikte' is an academic exemplar of Maya women's agency and creativity in attempting to shape substantively multicultural progressive efforts in the post-conflict era.

Formative experiences in a harshly assimilationist educational system coupled with later scholarly experiences dedicated to Maya cultural autonomy enabled Nikte' to enter the Achi-K'iche' debate as a native speaker and an expert linguist. Throughout the past decade, Nikte' has been embroiled in local and national debates about the status of Achi as a language or dialect. Recalling her early years as a fledgling student of linguistics, Nikte' described the shock she felt when she discovered that her native language, Achi, was classified as a dialect of K'iche' from a scientific perspective. "It caused me surprise to see," she remembered, "that Achi wasn't classified as a Mayan language. Dr. England explained that Achi was a variety of K'iche' and, for this reason, wasn't classified as a separate language" (Sis Iboy 2002:14).[5] Nikte' confesses that at the time of her initiation into academic linguistics, she didn't exactly understand the reasons for this distinction, because there were differences between the two varieties, especially at the lexical level (2002:14). Nikte's loyalty to her own community and to the views of other Achi speakers led her to take a clear-cut position on the debate she had been introduced to through her studies. Initially, Nikte' claimed that "Achi must be understood as a language in local ideological terms. Otherwise she would lose part of her cultural identity as an Achi" (2002:14).[6]

Turning this conflict into a scholarly investigation, Nikte' spent several years crafting empirical analyses of grammatical similarities and differences between K'iche' and Achi. With data from seventeen varieties of K'iche' and three varieties of Achi, she compared and contrasted phonological, morphological, and syntactic features of the varieties in *Ri K'ichee' Jay Ri Achi La E Ka'iib' Chi Ch'ab'al?* (K'iche' and Achi: Two Different Languages?). Nikte' begins the text by describing extensive grammatical similarities between the varieties at all levels of language structure. She then moves on to describe the structural differences between Achi and K'iche' and underscores that these data are key to defining the differences between a language and a dialect. At the level of sound, Nikte's analysis shows that both varieties share the same number of consonants and vowels—twenty-two of the former and ten of the latter—with only allophonic variation in the phonemes /q'/, /k/, /k'/, /w/, and /y/ (2002:146). Next, she shows that derivational morphology in both varieties is overwhelmingly isomorphic. The few exceptions she finds are the following suffixes: -V (found in only one variety of K'iche') and -i', -ichaal, -oy, -oq— found in all three Achi-speaking communities. Also at the morphological level, Nikte' notes differences in the use of the verbal root tajin- to mark progressive aspect. In K'iche' varieties, it functions as a particle and as an auxiliary verb, while in Achi varieties, it functions as a principal verb.[7] Her data on syntax in the seventeen varieties of K'iche' and three of Achi similarly elucidate minimal variation (2002:145–149).

Nikte' concludes her comparative grammatical analysis by arguing that the most substantive differences between Achi and K'iche' are at the lexical level. The linguistic evidence for this claim is derived from the collection of 1,500 words, including Swadesh's hundred-word list, an historical methodology often used in the comparative analysis of Mayan languages in Guatemala to ascertain degree of relatedness and time of separation (Kaufman 1974; England 1996; Mateo Toledo 1999; Sis Iboy 2002). When we consider Nikte's linguistic analysis relative to the phonetic and phonological analyses discussed in chapter 2, the flexibility of a disciplinary epistemology becomes clear. The unit of linguistic analysis changes with the political ends of the project. In this particular case, linguistic analysis shifts away from the earlier regimentation of sound and sound systems so crucial in the alphabet debates to scrutinize lexical forms. Nikte's emphasis on lexicon is intimately related to the privileging of semantico-referential intelligibility in the science of language (Silverstein 1976), as it has been inherited and practiced by structural Mayan linguistics in Guatemala.

With this orientation, Nikte' builds upon Swadesh's lexicostatistic methodology and Kaufman's advances in historical linguistics to show a wide range of time separation between the divergence of varieties of K'iche' and Achi. She marshals lexical data to show differences indicating from less than a century of divergence (the most closely related) to up to six centuries of divergence (the most distantly related). She concludes that a definitive time of separation between Achi and K'iche' cannot be determined precisely because of the vast range of variation within each of the two named varieties. Nikte' is quick to point out that the time range *between* K'iche' and Achi is equal to the range of time separation *within* the seventeen dialects of K'iche' (from no separation to five centuries) and within the three dialects of Achi (ranging from less than a century to five centuries). Nikte' uses these data to authoritatively conclude from a scholarly perspective that all varieties are, in fact, varieties of the same code—K'iche' (Sis Iboy 2002).

A Local Tradition and a Modern Political Future

Since 1994, Nikte' has spent several years presenting her data in local K'iche' and Achi communities, demonstrating how Maya linguists are committed to disseminating their findings to a variety of local, national, and international audiences. Nikte' reformulated her position as an expert native Achi speaker in a novel direction during 2002. Nikte's most recent intervention—formalized in *Ri K'ichee' Jay Ri Achi La E Ka'iib' Chi Ch'ab'al?*—rearticulates the tension between the science of linguistics and the tradition of a community in terms of a dual commitment to local demands for the recognition of difference and national calls for a collective sameness among Maya peoples. Nikte' argues:

> The linguists are right to say that Achi is a dialect of K'ichee'. The differences that exist in the forms of speech do not impede mutual intelligibility between speakers. This means that the differences are not so great as to mark them as different languages. Nevertheless, the Rabinal people have a history, a past as an independent people, an ethnic cultural identity that makes them feel different from other peoples. Based on this reality it is also understandable that they want their language [to be] recognized as different. (2002:15)

The position that Nikte' articulates, and that her OKMA colleagues support, resituates the tension between the science of language and the tradition of a community in terms of a double loyalty. It supports local demands for the recognition of particular historical tradition as well as supports national calls for the collective identification of a unified Maya pueblo. Nikte's position as an expert linguist and native speaker of Achi obtains in her bold new proposal: to rename the language variety from Achi to Rab'inalchii'. The new name would preserve the local identity by making a reference to place (the municipio of Rabinal), while the added "-chii'," functioning as a derivational suffix meaning mouth/language/word in K'iche' and Achi, would reference the language spoken in the community (the language of the Rabinal people). What is interesting in this proposal is not just the act of renaming a language variety, but also the particular strategy entailed by the act of renaming. The strategy that the new name follows is rooted in an explicitly comparative approach to Mayan linguistics and Maya peoples that stresses sameness among them. Using a locally meaningful word as a base followed by the suffix "-chii'" is consistent with the derivational morphology used to name other Mayan language varieties such as Q'eqchi', Poqomchii', Popti', and Ch'orti' (2002:158–159).

Comparative Linguistics and Pan-Maya Unification

Rab'inal + chii' (mouth/language/word)   Rab'inal*chii'*
Q'eq*chi'*
Poqom*chii'*
Pop*ti'*
Ch'or*ti'*

In addition to referencing a language spoken in a particular area, the proposed name change, if accepted by speakers and linguists, could function as a creative index of a new relationship between the ideologies of linguistic science and of linguistic tradition. More specifically, scientific linguistic epistemologies, instead of opposing local heterogeneity, can be mobilized to support difference. Epistemologies grounded in local tradition can be infused with new relations that orient the community outwards toward other Maya peoples and their languages.

This proposal shifts the terms of the debate from an either/or proposition and pushes deliberation to a new domain, where the possibility of arriving at a both/and perspective can obtain at least tentatively. Nikte's proposal performs a provisionally strategic solution that allows local identities to preserve their unique difference grounded in the tradition of the community *and* to contribute to the larger modernist project of Maya ethnolinguistic unification.

In fact, the manner in which Nikte's proposal brings scientifically supported ideologies of language into creative juxtaposition with traditionally grounded ones complicates Bauman and Briggs's (2003) theoretical account. Indeed, Bauman and Briggs posit that "tradition" and "modernity" have been constructed as oppositional forces in much social thought of the past three hundred years in ways that further social exclusions (2003:2). In Nikte's proposal, the modern and the traditional are dynamically brought together instead of opposed. The fusing of "modern" and "traditional" epistemologies evident in Nikte's intervention works in service of a more inclusive Guatemala and a potentially more unified Maya people, even as it refuses to exclude deeply held local perspectives on language and identity.

Modernity and Local Linguistic Ideologies in Chimaltenango

WHILE PAN-MAYA K'ICHE' linguists and local communities like the Achis negotiate "traditional" and modernist epistemologies and their relationships to competing versions of collective Maya identity, neighboring Kaqchikel linguists have similar, yet distinct, struggles. Of all Maya ethnolinguistic groups in Guatemala, Kaqchikel linguists have particular *fama* (notoriety) due to their organization, visibility, and leadership in the Maya movement. One of the historical conditions that provided the possibility for Kaqchikels' success is their intimate relationship with the hegemony of Spanish-speaking Ladino-dominated urban areas in colonial and contemporary times. Due to their close proximity to urban capitals like Antigua and Guatemala City, "Kaqchikels, to a greater extent than many other Maya groups of highland Guatemala, have been under heavy and constant pressure to adopt non-Indian ways, particularly in language" (Maxwell 1996:195). At the same time, Kaqchikels' close relationship to Ladino power centers has provided them with unusual access to educational opportunities in Spanish that many other indigenous groups have lacked. These unique circumstances make Kaqchikels "among the most highly educated Maya ethnolinguistic group in the highlands" (Maxwell 1996:195). North American secular linguist Judith Maxwell explains this trend: "Of the small cadre of Indians who have teaching certificates (a high school–level award), approximately 85 percent are Kaqchikels. Of the Kaqchikels finishing high school in 1988, 25 percent had some college-level training by 1990. This compares with less than 1 percent for other Indian ethnicities" (1996:195), like the Achi community from which Nikte' comes.

Faced with intense pressure to assimilate linguistically and culturally to Ladino ways, and simultaneously enabled to use a hegemonic education for counterhegemonic purposes, Kaqchikel linguists have also turned quite successfully to the science of linguistics in their struggle for cultural rights. Maxwell underscores: "There is now a relatively large corps of Kaqchikels who understand the structural complexities of their language, [who] not only can define a noun, a verb, and a positional but also know what makes their language an ergative one. They can describe and exemplify the passive and antipassive. All are committed to disseminating information about their language in *scientific* terms" (1996:197; emphasis mine). Several Kaqchikel linguists have become local, national, and international leaders in the Pan-Maya language and cultural unification project; in fact, it is their neologism efforts I discussed in chapter 1. Maxwell points out that in much of the current language revitalization efforts, "the central actors are Kaqchikel linguists who not only prepare materials in the language but can defend the language scientifically against outside denigration" (1996:198).[1] Indeed, as I have shown in chapter 2, scientific epistemology has been a powerful tool in authorizing and legitimizing Maya linguistic analyses in service of creating a more multicultural, multilingual, and multiethnic Guatemalan nation. As I will show, such an investment in modernist orientations is, in fact, shared by urban Kaqchikels not directly involved in Maya ethnonationalist efforts. However, local linguistic ideologies link Spanish with notions of modern personhood in ways that refract ideas of cultural tradition in new and unintended ways. More specifically, among some Mayas from the Chimaltenango area, Kaqchickel is contextually associated with a "premodern" cultural tradition that is perceptually distant even as it is a tradition newly revalued as part of collective identity in a "modern" context. In this way, the objectification of all Mayan languages, including Kaqchikel, as part of the Maya ethnolinguistic identity political project, serves to both valorize and reify collective cultural difference in circumscribed ways. Before discussing these grassroots ideologies of language and their relationships to modernity in more detail, I turn to discuss the ethnographic context and methodology from which the data (that I mentioned in the introduction) originate.

Chimaltenango and Language Shift

Chimaltenango is a city of transition, exchange, and industry. Officially known as Santa Ana Chimaltenango, Chimaltenango is the administrative and economic center of the department of Chimaltenango, encompassing sixteen *municipios*: Chimaltenango, Poaquil, San Martín, Comalapa, Santa Apolonia, Tecpán, Patzún, Pochuta, Patzicía, Balanyá, Acatenango, Yepocapa, Itzapa, Parramos, El Tejar, and Zaragoza. Figure 4 represents the state-defined political administrative unit of the Chimaltenango department that lies within ethnolinguistically defined boundaries of Kaqchikel peoples.

At the end of the twentieth century, the population of the Chimaltenango department was approximately 395,164 people (Instituto Nacional de Estadística 2009). The city's population began growing rapidly during The Violence, a time when many people fled from rural municipios, seeking refuge in the city (Powell 1989). As a result, many people live in Chimaltenango who are not originally from "the community." The population influx has been furthered by the city's location on the Pan-American Highway, which strategically links the burgeoning *maquila* (factory) garment industry with Guatemala City, the nation's capital, to the east.

While connections to capital lie in the east, Chimaltenango is also the gateway to the "Indian" highlands in the west. In fact, the department and its municipios are known in Guatemala for being very "Indian" (all municipios except Zaragoza are predominantly Kaqchikel communities), with a population that is roughly 80 percent indigenous and 20 percent Ladino (Hale 1996). Unlike other urban areas in the highlands, the city of Chimaltenango is unique in that Maya people rather than Ladinos are the majority of the population. In recent years, the city has become home to numerous Pan-Maya nongovernmental organizations (NGOs) like the Kaqchikel Cholchi', the organization that undertook the neologisms project I discussed in chapter 1. At the same time, Chimaltenango is a place where the economic and social forces of state-sponsored violence and late capitalism are visible through public commemorations for victims of the civil war, through numerous brothels along the highway, and through groups of youth gathering to take the bus to clothing factories owned by Korean entrepreneurs. Consequently, the city of Chimaltenango is also a locale where the economic, social, and political forces often influencing language shift from Kaqhickel to Spanish are dramatically embodied (Powell 1989; England 1998; Garzon 1998b). For these reasons, most Guatemalan linguists assume that Kaqchikel will no longer be spoken in

Municipalities of Chimaltenango

1   Tecpán Guatemala
2   Santa Apolonia
3   San José Poaquil
4   Comalapa
5   San Martín Jilotepeque
6   Patzún
7   Patzicía
8   Santa Cruz Balanyá
9   Zaragoza
10 Chimaltenango
11 El Tejar
12 Pochuta
13 Acatenango
14 San Andrés Itzapa
15 Parramos
16 Yepocapa

           Kaqchikel language area

Enlarged area

Figure 4. Chimaltenango department within Kaqchikel area (by Kathryn Dunn).

Chimaltenango within two generations. They often refer to Chimalte-nango as a community *ya perdida*, "already lost."

How, then, do these forces of modernity shape local bilingual ur-ban indigenous conceptualizations of Mayan languages (particularly Kaqchikel) and their relationships to notions of collective identity? Through an analysis of some urban indigenous Mayas' metalinguistic speech, I argue that a "discourse of progress" that links Kaqchikel with the "premodern" past is a particularly salient grassroots language ideology in the Chimaltenango area. A detailed analysis of the discourse of progress shows that, for this group of Mayas, the loss of Kaqchikel does not neces-sarily negate one's indigenous identity as essentialist constructs imply. Rather, it indicates a local reconfiguration of the language/collective identity relationship in nonessentialist terms.

As I have demonstrated in the initial chapters of this book, both the Guatemalan state and the Maya movement rely on language ideologies that link Mayan languages with essentialist constructions of Maya identity in their distinct political projects. In other words, Mayan languages hold a unique place among several aspects of culture that are objectified as the fundamental essences of Maya identity, the foundation upon which a col-lective identity, based upon difference within the nation, is erected. While both the Guatemalan state and the Maya movement are invested in propagating this nationalist language ideology, urban Maya-Kaqchikels from Chimaltenango are more explicitly invested in the perceived rela-tionships between language and modernity. This local concern with lan-guage and modernity, in turn, highlights the ethnographic saliency of Bauman and Briggs' theoretical preoccupation. In the pages that follow, I argue that this group of Mayas participates in the discourse of progress, a classificatory system made up of two constituent elements—the notion of the "premodern" past and the explicitly named "modern" present.[2] Lin-guistic ideologies of Spanish and Mayan languages provide the architec-ture of the system; they are the basis upon which the two homologous elements of the discourse of progress are erected. Kaqchikel indexes and ties together aspects of the premodern past, including parochialism, lack of formal education, and the hardship of poverty. Spanish indexes and ties together aspects of the modern present, including themes of worldliness, formal education, travel, and economic opportunities. These two con-structions, the premodern past and the modern present, structure the most salient language ideologies for those Maya people who participated in this study from the city of Chimaltenango and surrounding areas.

While these ordinary Maya-Kaqchikels produce the discourse of progress with language ideologies that link Kaqchikel to the premodern past and Spanish to the modern present, the data also show the presence of a supplementary discourse about Mayan languages. A simultaneous, emergent "discourse of culture" appears in informants' metalinguistic speech. The discourse of culture invokes respect for ancestral continuity in spoken Kaqchikel, for the historical perseverance of the language, and for contemporary Maya cultural activism. The supplementary discourse of culture produces an alternative linguistic ideology of Mayan languages, one that valorizes Mayan language for one specific aspect of identity. As we will see, this supplementary discourse of culture is evidence of an impact that the Maya movement has had on some Maya citizens in the Chimaltenango area. This is evident in that the discourse of culture articulates a new consciousness of the importance of Mayan languages to Pan-Maya ethnolinguistic identity. However, this additive discourse is not based upon an essentialized ideology linking language with a collective Maya peoplehood, as it is in Pan-Maya and state discourses. Rather, it reconfigures the importance of Mayan languages for one specific, compartmentalized, and objectified aspect of identity—"cultural" identity in the "modern" present. Taken together, the grassroots ideologies of language in Chimaltenango show the "partial, contradictory, fragile, unstable, and vulnerable" nature of hegemonies and counter-hegemonies (Gal 1998:321) in the construction of language and collective identity within a highly politicized national context. Before discussing the discourse of progress and the supplementary discourse of culture as they are structured by linguistic ideologies of Spanish and Mayan languages, I turn to provide a discussion of sociolinguistic interviews, the primary methodology used to collect the data upon which my analysis is based.

Sociolinguistic Interviews and Metalinguistic Speech

Because metalinguistic speech is a salient site where ideology directly impacts language (Woolard 1998), I self-consciously chose, in consultation with Oxlajuuj Keej Maya' Ajtz'iib' (OKMA) linguists, to elicit linguistic ideologies through the sociolinguistic interview. The interview is a familiar genre to many Mayas from Chimaltenango, precisely because "interviewing has become a powerful force in modern society" (Briggs 1986:1). Urban, mobile, Guatemalan Mayas tend to see themselves as new participants in the "modern" world; communicative knowledge of and competence with the interview indexes modernity as the genre proliferates in newspapers, magazines, radio programs, and television shows.

I presume that after the signing of the peace accords in 1996, the interview became even more prevalent in the discourse repertoires of many Guatemalans as hundreds of United Nations staff, social scientists, development coordinators, peace workers, and the like traversed the country to assess social conditions and implement a new democratic era in the nation. A barrage of authoritative professionals made these assessments through discourse, talking with the citizens and soliciting their perspectives on a variety of issues in interviews. One of many examples of the increased production of interviews in public discourse during my fieldwork was the government propaganda news report *Avances* (*Advancements*). *Avances* obligatorily aired nightly on all Guatemalan television channels during prime-time evening hours. It began programming during the presidency of Arzú, reporting on the new kinds of "progress" that the national government was making in the country. The show often began with a brief male voice-over on new "advancements" made in different Guatemalan communities. It then interviewed citizens, who were almost always Mayas, about their reactions to recent "advancements" in their rural villages and hamlets, like the development of infrastructure such as schools, potable water, and roads. Nightly, an omniscient, disembodied baritone voice announced that progress was arriving "even in the remotest areas of the country." Frequently, interviews with seemingly monolingual Ixil, K'iche', Mam, or Q'eqchi' women praised such new progress in their own native "dialects," which were then translated through subtitles into Spanish for the modern viewership in more urban environs.

Just as the government interviewed Mayas, so did a variety of foreign and domestic researchers. With literally millions of dollars pouring into Guatemala for democratization initiatives in the post–peace accords era from agencies such as United Nations and USAID (Warren 1998:62), international diplomats, researchers, and officials were a common presence in many highland communities. However varied their agendas, many researchers were interviewing Guatemalans, particularly Mayas, about their thoughts on various social issues. Indeed, it is possible to think of Maya representation in interviews as marking a potentially democratic opening of the public sphere, one that has until recently been closed to indigenous citizens. Because of this recent proliferation of interviews in the public sphere and Mayas' increasing participation in them, the sociolinguistic interview was a particularly appropriate genre and method for discerning explicit grassroots language ideologies.

My bilingual Maya research assistant Miriam Rodríguez and I interviewed 128 individuals in the sociolinguistic survey. Our sampling was opportunistic; we surveyed people who agreed to talk with us in the mornings and afternoons during the week and on weekends. We conducted most of the interviews in public spaces such as the market, small *tiendas*, and the central park. In a few cases when I knew the respondents, surveys were conducted in their homes. The population represents urban-working and -dwelling individuals who were more likely than rural populations to rely on Spanish in their daily activities. These people were more integrated into cash-generating activities such as vending and wage labor, which necessitated that they understood and used Spanish more than individuals involved primarily in subsistence activities in surrounding rural areas. Given the small size of the sample, a larger random sample would be necessary to confirm the trends in the data that are discussed below.

The demographics of the sample population reflect the heterogeneity of the Chimaltenango population. Only 44 percent of respondents were originally from the city of Chimaltenango. An additional 25.2 percent of participants were originally from other Chimaltenango municipios, particularly Comalapa, Tecpán, Poaquil, San Martín, Pochuta, and Patzicía.[3] Another 13.4 percent of respondents were from an *aldea* in the department, and 11 percent were from K'iche'-speaking departments, mostly El Quiché and Totonicapán. The remaining 6.4 percent were from elsewhere in Guatemala.

Those who spoke with us represented a broad age range; the youngest participant was twelve years old and the oldest was seventy-seven. The majority of people who talked with us were young. People ages twenty to twenty-nine comprised 28.3 percent of the respondents. The next largest group was teenagers, twelve to nineteen years old, which comprised 18.9

percent of the respondents. The sample is not particularly skewed toward a younger generation; in fact, it mirrors the demographic composition of the country. An estimated 51.6 percent of Guatemala's population of 10.3 million was under the age of eighteen at the end of the twentieth century (Casa Alianza 2000). Of the respondents, 16.5 percent were between the ages of thirty and thirty-nine, with another 15 percent of respondents representing ages forty to forty-nine. The remaining individuals who participated were in the age groups of fifty to fifty-nine, sixty to sixty-nine, and seventy to seventy-nine, each group constituting 7.1 percent of the survey population. Seventy-six women and fifty-two men participated in our study, constituting 59.3 and 40.6 percent of the survey population, respectively.

The vast majority of our respondents were people involved in wage labor activities and had little formal education. About 89.8 percent of respondents worked in the market, in the home (their own or someone else's), in the field, and/or in the factory. Only 10.2 percent were students or had professional occupations. Most of the individuals were not directly involved in the Pan-Maya movement, as most Pan-Maya activists have professional jobs in the government or NGOs.

All of the surveys (except three) were conducted in Spanish; this was neither by necessity nor design. My competency in Kaqchikel was not adequate for collecting interviews in the language, but Miriam's competency was, because she is a native speaker of both Spanish and Kaqchikel. For this reason, we decided that I would work in Spanish and she would attempt to work in Kaqchikel. Miriam, who worked for decades in the market as a successful vendor to both Ladinos and Mayas, had a keen sense of the semiotic indicators of indigenous identity, so I left it to her to decide with whom she would speak Kaqchikel in contexts she felt appropriate. To the surprise of us both, even individuals who spoke Spanish seemingly as a second language were extremely reluctant to speak Kaqchikel. Frequently, Miriam would begin an interview with a greeting in Kaqchikel and the respondent would code-switch immediately to Spanish. Miriam's normative sense was that to not respond in Spanish would be rude, perhaps even insulting.[4] Thus, Miriam never collected any of the data entirely in Kaqchikel, even with bilinguals from her hometown of Tecpán, with whom she would have presumably shared a common notion of local Maya identity.

The sanctioning against Kaqchikel as a highly marked, problematic code in public discourse in Chimaltenango reoccurred in a variety of quotidian interactions in which I took part or witnessed. In fact, over the course of the research project, I became very preoccupied with the lack of "good" data in Kaqchikel; Miriam and I spent many hours discussing it. My concern that neither Miriam nor I could elicit discourse in Kaqchikel, as well as Chimaltecos' persistent desire to use Spanish exclusively in the interview context, are ideologically loaded facts. Indeed, the disciplinary linguistic ideologies of my scholarly training tend to situate indigenous languages like Kaqchikel as more "authentic" than dominant languages like Spanish among native communities. Bucholtz has recently critiqued this scholarly linguistic ideology, what she calls "the sociolinguistic invest-ment in authenticity," by which linguistic anthropologists and sociolingu-ists working with endangered language groups tend to privilege the dis-course of monolingual "native" language speakers (2003:398–399). From this professional ideological perspective, bilingual speakers or mono-lingual speakers in the hegemonic language who cannot or will not pro-duce the endangered language are perceived to be illegitimate representa-tives of a given community (2003:400). Thus, our work in Chimaltenango with bilingual and Spanish monolingual indigenous people serves to challenge notions of essentialized "authenticity" in representations of contemporary Maya peoples that circulate in U.S. academic as well as Pan-Maya intellectual communities. In fact, these particular Chimaltecos publicly identify as indigenous even as they are becoming rapidly mono-lingual in Spanish, a point that merits further discussion below.

In this context, it is important to underscore that neither Miriam nor I encountered any strictly monolingual Kaqchikel speakers during our work in the Chimaltenango department or city. Only one person in our entire survey reported that he had children who did not know Spanish—a farmer who lived in an aldea of the neighboring department, Sololá. Nevertheless, every person who participated in our survey reported that at least some member or members of their family—grandparents, parents, or themselves—were speakers of a Mayan language. Kaqchikel was rep-resented most as the language of one's family background. One hun-dred and eight people had speakers of Kaqchikel in their family, and K'iche' was the familial language reported by seventeen people. Speakers of Q'eqchi' and Tz'utujiil were also represented in our data.[5]

The Discourse of Progress:
The "Premodern" Past and "Modern" Present

Overall, a collective notion about progress—a commonplace idea about the way things seem to have recently changed for the better in the lives of this group of predominantly Kaqchikel Mayas—emerges in metalinguistic talk. The "discourse of progress" is made up of two interrelated constructs, the "premodern" past and the "modern" present, made up of clusters of reoccurring themes. The discourse of the premodern past linked with Kaqchikel is constituted by the themes of (1) parochialism, (2) a lack of formal education, (3) isolated living conditions, and (4) the hardship of poverty. The conception of the "modern" present linked with Spanish is characterized by (1) worldliness, (2) formal education, (3) travel and migration, and (4) economic opportunity. Taken together, these elements weave a discourse about progress. Their constituent themes and association with Spanish and Kaqchikel emerged repeatedly in metalinguistic speech from 128 participants. To be sure, not every person mentioned all of the themes, nor were these themes always connected in as coherent a manner as I represent them here. Nevertheless, a majority (more than seventy) of the respondents discussed constituent elements of both discourses.[6] The discourse of progress and its associated language ideologies among these Kaqchikel Mayas form "a discursive system whose coherence becomes discernible through metalinguistic talk," much like Hill's analysis of linguistic ideologies and nostalgia among indigenous Mexicano speakers (1998). Indeed, the discourse of progress and its constituent parts emerged in the context of explicit talk about languages in the following patterned ways. First, the discourses of the premodern past and the modern present are syntagmatically chained in speakers' talk about Spanish and Mayan languages. Second, there is a relational contrast between the premodern past and the modern present, often recursively projected (Irvine and Gal 2000) onto a contrast between Kaqchikel and Spanish. Third, talk about Spanish and Mayan languages functions as a "multiplex sign," which Hill defines by drawing on the work of Briggs (1989) as "elements that not only refer to, but call up indexically an entire social order" (1998:71). Therefore, as a structured discursive system, the discourse of progress invokes, in metalinguistic talk about Spanish and Mayan languages, ideas about the premodern past and the modern present as an integral part of the practical consciousness (Williams 1977) of its speakers. Social actors' lived experiences with multilingualism, collective identity, and modernity in the urban highlands of Guatemala give rise to these ideologies of language.

Relational Constructs: A Kaqchikel Past, A Spanish Present

As will be made clear below, in the discourse of progress, the premodern past is linked with Kaqchikel and the modern present is linked with Spanish. As the example below demonstrates, Spanish and Kaqchikel (and other Mayan languages) are relationally understood and classified. A thirty-year-old bilingual market woman from Chimaltenango explained to Miriam:

1) Últimamente están hablando más el español. Ya el kaqchikel, casi ya
   Lately they are speaking more Spanish. Now, Kaqchikel, now, hardly
2) ya no.
   at all.

An association between the distant past with Kaqchikel and the contemporary present with Spanish through temporal adverbs (lines 1–2) is constructed through this woman's metalinguistic talk. Such talk brings these relations between language and perception of time into the interviewee's consciousness. Similar connections were echoed by many of our respondents, including a fifty-five-year old bilingual market man from Chimaltenango. He said:

3) Mucho antes sí había bastantes, [hablantes de Kaqchikel],
   A long time ago, yeah, there were many [Kaqchikel speakers],
4) pero, ahora ya no.
   but now, not anymore.

In metalinguistic speech, Spanish is associated with the present, marked commonly in talk by temporal markers such as "últimamente" (line 1) and "ahora" (line 4) and progressive verbs like "están hablando" (line 1). In contrast, Kaqchickel is associated with the past. Temporal markers such as "mucho antes" (line 3) and verb tenses like the imperfect "había" (line 3) situate Kaqchikel as a language that was spoken by many people long ago for an extended period of time, but which now is a language that has become almost implicitly obsolete in the present (as indicated by "ya no" [line 4]).

In addition to associating Kaqchikel with the past and Spanish with the present in her metalinguistic speech, a sixteen-year-old monolingual Spanish-speaking woman who worked as a clerk in a bookstore specified the present as the time of modernity. She implied with a relative claim that the past was not yet modern in the Chimaltenango region. When I asked her the seemingly banal question, "What communities speak Kaqchikel in the Chimaltengo department?" her response completely subverted my geographical frame. Instead of talking about Kaqchikel speakers in local areas, the young clerk responded by discussing Spanish and modernity:

5) Pues, el español, es más, más, como le diré (1), moderno, ¿verdad?
   Well, Spanish, is more, more, how should I say, modern, right?

This young woman's metalinguistic remark highlights the relational construct between Mayan languages and Spanish as evidenced in her use of the comparative "más" in line 5. As was frequently the case in sociolinguistic interviews as well as in quotidian discussions, a question about Kaqchikel precipitated commentary about Spanish. Furthermore, the young clerk's answer highlights the comparative linking of Spanish with the modern contemporary moment and Kaqchikel with its antithesis—the premodern past. She concludes her point by supposing agreement with the tag question "¿verdad?" in line 5 about this seemingly commonsensical knowledge about Spanish and Kaqchikel. Relational constructs between Spanish and Kaqchikel are set in place through the use of verb tenses, temporal expressions, and comparatives.

Syntagmatic Chaining

In addition to interviewees' metalinguistic talk engendering a connection between Mayan languages and the premodern past as well as a connection between Spanish and the modern present, there are two more constituent elements of the discourse of progress—syntagmatic chaining and multiplex signs. The frequent syntagmatic chaining of Spanish and Mayan languages in metalinguistic speech occurs with a few specific and limited themes. This means that specific themes emerge together in discourse (appear together on the syntagmatic axis) with talk about the two languages (Hill 1998). For example, a speaker may mention Spanish and immediately begin talking about access to technology. Spanish is regularly syntagmatically chained in discourse with themes of formal education, social sophistication, travel and migration, and economic advancement. Mayan languages are syntagmatically chained in Chimaltecos' discourse with lack of formal education, social provincialism, rural life, and poverty. This syntagmatic chaining appeared in several interviews, including in the response of a forty-eight-year-old market woman who was bilingual in Spanish and Kaqchikel. The woman, originally from Tecpán, had migrated to Chimaltenango. She responded to Miriam's question, "In what municipios of Chimaltenango is Kaqchikel spoken?" with the following discussion of ignorance and worldliness.

6) Pues, ahora yo, yo veo que todo la mayoría ahora ya sabe [hablar en
   Well, now I, I see that all of the majority, now already know [how
7) español] porque ahora ya no es ignorante la gente como antes.
   to speak Spanish], because now the people aren't ignorant like before.
8) Si pues, ya casi están despertando, ¿verdad? No como nosotros, nos
   Well, now they are almost waking up, right? Not like us
9) crecimos, más, más, nuestras papás, pues. Ahora ya no.
   who grew up, more, more, well, like our parents. Now, not anymore.
10) Porque antes, se la gente pues, ellos se esconden—¿verdad?—
    Because before, the people, well, they, hide themselves—right?—
11) que tenían miedo de los gringos. Pero ahora ya no.
    they were afraid of the gringos. But now, not anymore.

Like others, this woman links the past with Kaqchikel and the present with Spanish, stressing "ahora," a temporal link, in lines 6, 7, and 9. Additionally, she elaborates on "life in the past" by explaining that people used to be ignorant—thereby associating social ignorance with speaking Kaqchikel ("now the people aren't ignorant like before" in line 7).

While the premodern past and the modern present are often constructed in metalinguistic discourse as discrete historical times, in this woman's speech, the boundaries become blurred. While she reveals her own experience of these "past ways," her discourse shows efforts to identify with life in the modern present. In line 7, she explains how people used to be ignorant and begins to include herself in the "we" of this group, saying "not like us who grew up" (lines 8–9). Here she hesitates, then repeats herself, as she searches for an explanation ("más, más" in line 9). She concludes by removing herself from this experience, asserting that it is older people, like "our parents" (line 9), who grew up in this premodern way.[7] In addition to shifting her positionality in relation to the experience of modernity she recounted, the woman shifts times in her account. She talks about the past way of life, marked by the use of "antes" (line 7), but slips into the present tense when she explains how people hide, "Se esconden" ("they hide"). Again, she quickly reverts to the historical past, marked by the imperfect verb tense, when people "hid themselves" from the gringos (lines 10–11).

As this woman reproduces a linguistic ideology linking the premodern past with Kaqchikel and the modern present with Spanish, she continues to articulate more thematic elements of the discourse of progress. In particular, these are ideas about mobility and technology that are expressed through syntagmatic chaining and are related to difference between how life is imagined in the modern present and how it may have been in the premodern past. This bilingual market woman continues to associate these elements with her explanations about why people don't speak in Kaqchikel anymore:

12) Ya no pues, porque ya sale y la televisión. Aunque
    Now no because they get out and the television. Even if they
13) sea tan pobre de una vez, tiene su televisión.
    are really poor, they still have their television.

In her metalinguistic discourse, this woman links the perceived demise of Kaqchikel with present opportunities to leave one's community, explaining, "They get out/they leave" (line 12), and also with access to technological advances, like the television (lines 12–13). Talk of such opportunities and technologies is conveyed in the present tense and associated with Spanish in the contemporary "modern" moment. She elaborates in another part of her discussion:

14) Hay que amar lo más sencillo. Hay que amarlo.
    One has to love the simplest people, one has to love them.
15) Hay que, tal vez, hay una cosa que necesita o digamos, uno tiene
    One has to, perhaps, someone needs something or say, one is

16) hambre, se encuentra una persona que es sencilla y que no
    hungry, one encounters a person that is simple and who doesn't
17) entiende como hablar, tienes que hablar en lengua.
    understand how to speak, you have to speak to them in the indigenous
    language.

This middle-aged market woman uses the "modern" Spanish code along with a distinctly Maya-style discourse feature—repetition—to make moral claims about how to treat "simple" people (line 14). She explains that one must be compassionate with those kinds of people and speak in Kaqchikel to them (lines 16–17). In this common perspective, Spanish is the un-marked, taken-for-granted language that one normally uses to communi-cate in the "modern" present, even as—at least in this woman's speech—discourse structures commonly deployed in Mayan languages (Brody 1986) are used to convey this ideology. In this way, the woman shows how speaking in Spanish becomes chained with technological advances and travel in the present. From her perspective, speaking in Kaqchikel has been a moral choice to assist those Maya people less fortunate.

During our interviews, similar themes and ideological connections appeared repeatedly in Chimaltecos' metalinguistic talk. Consider the relational comparisons between Spanish and Kaqchikel made in the fol-lowing examples from some respondents who reflected on their own language abilities. A twenty-year-old bilingual maid explained to Miriam the power of Spanish in the following way:

18) Español le saca a uno de un lado retirado. Lo sacan (a uno).
    Spanish takes one out of a remote, isolated place. It takes one out.
19) Se va por un lado, o maneras que lo hace uno, por uno sabiendo hablar.
    One leaves for another place, or, it is a way for one to do it, knowing how
    to talk.

For this young woman, as for many others, Spanish is perceived to be the agent (not the instrument) for removing someone from an undesirable, remote place and an isolated way of living. Spanish is the grammatical agent of the sentence (line 18) and literally acquires agency over people—a way of acting upon them in a manner that is perceived to be advantageous.

Another example of the syntagmatic chaining of Kaqchikel with themes of the "traditional" past and Spanish with the "modern" present occurred in the words of a thirty-year-old market woman originally from Chimaltenango. She reflected on her own bilingualism in Spanish and Kaqchikel:

20) Yo puedo comunicar con la gente de la más remota comunidad así,
   I can communicate with the people from the most remote community
21) como también, con los más altos ejecutivos porque hablo las dos
   as well as with the highest executives because I speak
22) cosas, kaqchikel y español.
   both, Kaqchikel and Spanish.

As with the ideologies expressed by many other respondents, Kaqchikel is here explicitly and commonly associated with aspects of a bygone way of life, such as living in an isolated area—as is expressed in line 20 ("the most remote community"). The presupposition here is that one would actually need to speak Kaqchikel only when dealing with people that live in such an isolated area. From this commonplace perspective, Spanish remains unmarked as the taken-for-granted code of quotidian life. Among our Chimalteco respondents, talk about Spanish unfolded in discourse next to ideals of education and wealth, as expressed by this woman in line 21 with "the highest executives."

Similar ideological notions were conveyed by a fifty-five-year-old bilingual man working as a marketer and an occasional driver for hire. He commented to Miriam on his ability to speak Spanish:

23) Se puede conversar con gentes ladinos así todos,
   One can communicate with ladinos, all kinds of people,
24) licenciados, un doctor, uno va a entender.
   degreed professionals, a doctor, and one will understand.

As in most of our metalinguistic data, Spanish is chained with both high levels of formal education and economic advancement. The bilingual woman quoted above immediately linked speaking Kaqchikel with interacting with a person from a rural isolated community, and she linked Spanish with high-ranking executives. The marketer/driver similarly represented Spanish as the language of educated and wealthy people, most often Ladinos, like doctors and *licenciados* (graduated university professionals).[8] In the context of metalinguistic discourse, to speak of economic advancement and educational opportunities in Guatemala is to speak of Spanish.

Multiplex Signs: Kaqchikel and Spanish

The third element of the discourse of progress is the way in which named linguistic codes become multiplex signs. The lexemes "Kaqchikel" and "Spanish" function not only referentially, to denote particular languages, but also indexically, to invoke an entire way of life. Hill explains that multiplex signs permit speakers to move from one thematic element to another in discourse without bridging argumentation between them (1998:72). When discussing Kaqchikel during an interview, a sixty-five-year-old Spanish monolingual market woman from Chimaltenango situated the historical perseverance of the Kaqchikel language in relation to a particular way of life. She explained to Miriam:

25) Bueno, muchas [personas van a hablar Kaqchikel] porque los que
    Well, many [people will still speak Kaqchikel] because those who
26) son de aldea no dejan de vivir así.
    are from the remote rural areas don't stop living like that.

This example illustrates that the code "Kaqchikel" functions as a multiplex sign—to speak of Kaqchikel is to invoke an entire way of life that, from this woman's perspective at least, is practiced by people who live in aldeas—small, remote, rural hamlets. In this instance, talk about the linguistic code, Kaqchikel, invokes a distinct manner of living, a particular place, and a certain way of life. For this market woman and others in urban Chimaltenango at the end of the twentieth century, metalinguistic discourse about Kaqchikel brings forth immediate associations with people who continue to live "like that" (line 26). This conceptualization also suggests that when people stop living the way of life associated with rural, isolated communities, Kaqchikel will no longer be spoken. The way of life and the language it indexes seem so interwoven that one cannot be spoken of without the other.

A more elaborate version of "the way of life" associated with Kaqchikel is represented in the words of a forty-three-year-old bilingual man from San Martín who managed a local office. For him, to talk about Kaqchikel is to invoke a concrete and undesirable way of life that he experienced as a youth in the past. He explained to me:

27) Por ejemplo, en que sí están realmente, de los que sí están, están
    For example, those who are really, those who are, are

28) directamente todo pueblo indígena, que, que (1) comparten
    directly in a total indigenous community, they share

29) la misma cultura, la misma creencia, ellos están unidos.
    the same culture, the same beliefs, they are united.

30) Pero entre los que salieron fuera de este carril,
    But for those who already left this track,

31) ya es un poco difícil meternos nuevamente.
    it is a bit difficult for us to get into it again.

32) Por ejemplo, el indígena está acostumbrado
    For example, the indigenous person is accustomed to

33) todo, todo, en lo pobre. Todo, todo, aunque
    everything, everything in poverty. Everything, everything, even if he

34) tenga dinero pero está acostumbrado a hacer sus cosas.
    has money but he still is accustomed to doing his things.

35) Ya no usa, por ejemplo, cosas aparatosas,
    He doesn't use, for example, gadgets

36) y en su forma de hablar, su forma de comportarse
    and in his way of speaking, in his way of behaving

37) entonces esto va directamente en su pequeño grupo que
    so all of this fits directly in his small group that

38) allí se llevan, se comprenden, hablan, platican,
    there they all get along, they understand each other, they speak, they talk

39) las necesidades, las mismas necesidades, comparten las mismas necesidades
    the necessities, the same necessities, they share the same necessities

40) comparten los mismos paraísos, comparten todo.
    they share the same paradises, they share everything.

41) Ya es, es, un cambio de vida, directamente, bastante.
    Now, it's, it's a direct and strong change of life.

42) Ya, ya llegó a modernismo. Entonces, el que llega a modernismo
    Now, now modernism arrived. So, he who arrives at modernism

43) ya no quiere regresar a su, su época.
    now does not want to return to his, his epoch.

44) Y si no quiere regresar a su época,
    And if he does not want to return to his epoch,

45) ya no quiere regresar a su cultura.
     now he does not want to return to his culture.
46) Ya no quería regresar a su idioma.
     Now he would not want to return to his language.
47) Ya no quería, ya no le gustaría andar con ciates,
     Now he would not want, now he would not like to walk in native sandals
48) ya no le gustaría andar con sandalias,
     now he wouldn't like to walk around in sandals,
49) ya no le gusta el corte de pelo, su comportamiento.
     now he doesn't like the hair cut, his behavior.
50) En cuanto a ellos están todavía enfocado en todo,
     Regarding those who are still focused on everything,
51) están acostumbrados a todo de este sistema de vida.
     they are accustomed to everything in this way of life.

In the above perspective, "Kaqchikel" functions as a sign that not only refers to a specific code, but also functions indexically to invoke an entire way of life. It is a life in which the community of speakers is nostalgically remembered as unified, an association rhetorically highlighted through the extensive use of parallelism (lines 29, 36, 39–40, 43–44, 45–47) and repetition (lines 33 and 39). Despite the nostalgia, to speak of the imagined bygone days of community unification is to recall several other aspects of daily life in the community that are not valued by the speaker. This adult man and others like him see the "way of life" linked to Kaqchikel as a premodern, traditional, impoverished existence in rural highland indigenous communities. He explains that the indigenous man living in an indigenous community is "accustomed to everything in poverty . . . even if he has money" (lines 32–34). It is a manner of living that undergoes a dramatic and systemic change with the advent of modernity, a "change of life" that transforms everything when modernism arrives (line 42). The resulting change is constructed as both desirable and irreversible: "He . . . does not want to return to his epoch. And if he does not want to return to his epoch, now he does not want to return to his culture. Now he would not want to return to his language [Kaqchikel]" (lines 43–46). Ideologically, this means that the indigenous person who seeks to escape the kind of life associated with the economic and social marginalization of Maya peoples will no longer want to speak Kaqchikel, even as it may mean losing a sense of community unity and solidarity.

Language Ideologies and "Modern" Personhood

Maya citizens of Chimaltenango identify themselves as actors in a "modern" present within which life is perceived to be materially, economically, and socially better than it had been in the past, before their entrance into "modernity." Their language ideologies link Kaqchikel with undesirable, old ways of living, and Spanish with modern, desirable ones. This linking encourages linguistic assimilation and expedites language shift in that it implicitly makes speaking Spanish and Kaqchikel mutually exclusive practices, in which the former is desirable and the latter is not. Thus, the ideology of exclusivity discussed in chapter 1, which was imposed by powerful Guatemalan institutions—like the military and the educational system—upon highland K'iche' and Kaqchikel communities, is re-created in the metalinguistic speech of some bilingual, urban Chimaltecos.

As I demonstrated in chapters 1 and 2, the Guatemalan state and Ladino intellectuals have promoted the notion that as Mayas become integrated into a capitalist economy and the modern nation-state, their languages and cultures will disappear. In other words, their marked difference will be transformed into national linguistic and cultural sameness. In this hegemonic assimilationist model of nation building, to become "modern" is to become a Spanish-speaking Guatemalan instead of a Mayan-speaking "Indian."[9] This relational, indexical linking of Kaqchikel with premodernity and Spanish with modernity empirically supports the kind of hegemonic social formulation that Bauman and Briggs (2003) theorize in their historical analysis of language ideologies, modernity, and inequality. In this ethnographic instance, the language ideologies among bilingual urban Mayas in the Chimaltenango area confirm the powerful dichotomy that Bauman and Briggs argue structures inequality, namely "a general pair of associational complexes that resonate strongly . . . rural (or aboriginal), lower class, ignorant, old-fashioned, indigenous—in a word, *provincial*—versus urban, elite, learned, cosmopolitan, that is to say, *modern*" (2003; emphasis in original).

However, this commonplace ideology—that "Indian" identity will be gradually erased as Mayas speak Spanish and become "modern" Guatemalans—is simultaneously problematized by the language ideologies and collective identifications of some Chimaltecos. Metalinguistic discourse among the urban Chimaltecos with whom Miriam and I spoke simultaneously shows the partialness of, and play in, the hegemony of modernity. While Mayas of Chimaltenango explicitly produced language ideologies that promote Spanish linguistic assimilation, their identification with a collective "modern" yet distinctly indigenous identity was simultaneously articulated. In other words, their metalinguistic discourse also shows moments of a "transitory, delicate, and momentary phase of social change" (Voloshinov 1973:19). These moments of delicate social change are related to Pan-Maya linguistic and cultural activism in the peace-accords era.

Despite their claims to Spanish/Kaqchikel bilingualism or Spanish monolingualism, several of the Chimaltecos we interviewed understood themselves as belonging to a collective identity that was marked as oppositional to Ladino identity. References to a collective, exclusive "we" often emerged in Chimaltectos' metalinguistic speech. For example, one seventy-three-year-old bilingual man from Comalapa living in Chimaltenango explained the following about Spanish:

52) Fíjese usted, si solo los Ladinos van por arriba, no sirve.
   See here, if only the Ladinos are on top, it's no good.
53) Hay que (1) levantarse a mismos nosotros. Por eso es que
   We have to get up there ourselves. That's why
54) ha superado Guatemala, porque ahora hablan español,
   Guatemala has improved, because now many people speak Spanish,
55) muchos (2) muchos estudios.
   a lot a lot of studying.

For many people like this elderly man, the collective "we" of indigenous Mayas, used in the plural pronoun "ourselves" (line 53), represents a collectivity that can be maintained without necessarily speaking Mayan languages. Here, the collective "we" stands in opposition to "Ladinos" in line 52 of the example above. From this perspective, embracing Spanish should not necessarily be conflated with a change in one's identity from indigenous to nonindigenous. Rather, a shift to Spanish is frequently conceptualized as a tool that Mayas learn and master so as to make an entrance into the modern present, where a better way of life is presumed to be waiting. The man quoted above metaphorically speaks of progress as "van por arriba" ("getting ahead") (line 52) and attributes improvements in Guatemala to the many people who learned to speak Spanish through education (lines 53–54), much like Don Fidencio, who admired Spanish acquisition among members of his natal community even under highly fraught conditions. From this perspective, using Spanish as a ladder in order to climb upward to the vistas of progress often means that Mayan languages are left behind, at the bottom of the ladder.

While such an idea instantiates the hegemony of modernity, it does so incompletely. Collective Maya identity is not erased in the service of a collective Guatemalan one. Nowhere in the data was the notion articulated that collective identification as Maya people must be relinquished so that the climb upward to progress may be successful. In fact, all the people who participated in this study acknowledged that Mayan languages were in their familial or individual backgrounds, and therefore they were not invested in "passing as Ladinos" in public contexts.[10] Furthermore, all of the women represented in the data were wearing some indigenous clothing, publicly marking themselves as Maya women, a point I take up in detail in the following chapter.[11] This suggests that the disuse of Kaqchikel (and other Mayan languages) should not be unilaterally equated with a negation of indigeneity in ways that essentialist constructions imply.[12] Rather, the claimed disuse of Kaqchikel can be understood as a way of distancing oneself from a particular way of life indexically linked with the language. As I've shown above, the way of life that Kaqchikel indexes is an economically, materially, and educationally difficult one. These Chimaltecos' act of distancing is intimately tied to the modernist discourse of progress in which the modern present, in contrast to the premodern past, is positively evaluated in terms of economic opportunities, formal education, and cosmopolitanism. The language ideologies linking Spanish with the modern present and Kaqchikel with the premodern past are the nexus of the discursive system of progress.

While distancing oneself from Kaqchikel is certainly hegemonic, it is not an absolute negation of indigenous identity, as is commonly assumed by essentializing political projects. I now turn to discuss how the discourse of progress is disrupted by what I call a supplementary discourse of culture. As we will see, Mayan languages become new and important objectified representations of culture for some modern Chimaltecos in the post-conflict era.

A Supplementary Discourse: Culture Talk

While the discourse of progress is a dominant discourse among this particular group of Maya-Kaqchikels, it is not a seamless one. In explor-
ing the metalinguistic data presented in this book, another discourse
emerged alongside the discourse of progress: the discourse of culture.
Through the discourse of culture, language is invoked as a unique possession of a collective Maya people. In it, language becomes "the objectified
matter that stands for the inherent goodness, value, and praiseworthiness
of a collective group within the modern nation-state" (Domínguez and
Welland 1998:12). The discourse of culture supplements the discourse of
progress and, in so doing, functions disruptively in the way that Bhabha
claims marginal discourses do:

> The strategy [of minority discourses] is what parliamentary procedure
> recognizes as a supplementary question. It is a question that is supple-
> mentary to what is put down on the order paper, but by being "after" the
> original, or in "addition to," it gives the advantage of introducing a sense
> of "secondariness" or belatedness into the structure of the original. The
> supplementary strategy suggests that adding "to" need not "add up" but
> may disturb the calculation. (1992:305)

This supplementary discourse of culture disrupts the binary calculations
of Kaqchikel with an undesirable past and disrupts Spanish with a valued present and future. More specifically, in the discourse of culture,
Kaqchikel is invested with associations of a familiar heritage in the past
and a cultural distinctiveness in the present. Through these affirma-
tive valuations of Kaqchikel in imagined past and present moments, the
discourse of culture unsettles the dominant ideological associations of
Kaqchikel that situate it as a language left behind in times and places in
existence before modernity arrived. As I will show, the disruption of the
discourse of progress by the discourse of culture can be attributed to the
language ideological work of Pan-Maya activists and scholars. While the
constituent themes of the discourse of culture occur less frequently than
the themes of the discourse of progress, the former re-entextualizes Pan-
Maya notions of ethnolinguistic identification within local Chimaltecos'
speech. Discerning thematic, linguistic, and intertextual elements of the
discourse of culture, therefore, is key to identifying the effects that Pan-

Maya activists have had on the language ideologies of ordinary Maya citizens in the urban highland areas of Chimaltenango.

This discourse of culture and the language ideologies it promotes emerge in three recurring themes in Chimaltecos' metalinguistic talk: (1) familial and ancestral use of Kaqchikel, (2) the deep historical presence of the Kaqchikel language in indigenous communities, and (3) contemporary Pan-Maya cultural revitalization that valorizes all Mayan languages in an ethnonationalistic sense. Together, these three elements link Mayan languages with a unique cultural distinctiveness belonging to a unified Maya people reconfigured for participation in the Guatemalan national community in the post-conflict era.

The first theme, familial and ancestral use of Kaqchikel, was present in the majority of the data. For example, a twenty-year-old bilingual maid from Chimaltenango respectfully discussed with Miriam those people who still speak Kaqchikel well. She said:

56) Los gentes ya (1), más grandes que (1), ellos hablan más,
    The people who are older than, they speak more,
57) que tienen experiencia de las palabras de antes que ya tienen ellos.
    they have experience with the words from the past, that they still have.

This woman speaks of "los gentes más grandes" ("the older people," line 56) who have a knowledge and experience of the old ways of speaking ("las palabras de antes," line 57). It is a knowledge that younger people apparently lack, expressed in the comparative "más" ("more") in line 56.

In addition to "gentes más grandes," there are a variety of terms that the majority of respondents used in reference to Kaqchikel speakers. They include:

58) los viejitos	the little old people
59) gente de nosotros	our people
60) nuestros abuelos	our grandparents
61) la gente anciana	the old people
62) nuestros papás	our parents
63) los antepasados	the ancestors

These phrases are kinship and generational terms that mark speakers' affect for family members. "Los viejitos" ("the little old people" in line 58) and "la gente anciana" ("the old people" in line 61) affectionately and respectfully refer to very old living people, while terms like "los ante-pasados" ("the ancestors" in line 63) refer to more temporally distant kin who have passed on. Uses of these terms situate Kaqchikel as the language of older generations, both living and dead, who belong to the families of these Chimaltecos.

Kin and generation terms are used in conjunction with first-person plural pronouns to explicitly articulate a sense of collective distinctiveness and to engender a continuity of self-expressed familial identifications, implying a shared collective history of Kaqchikel usage. For example, oftentimes these terms are marked with the plural possessive "our," a referential index (Silverstein 1976) that, in this case, functions to include the speaker and the referent in the same social group. In this way, plural possession of terms like "our parents" ("nuestros papás" in line 62) and "our grandparents" ("nuestros abuelos" in line 60) identify the speaker with older people who speak/spoke Kaqchikel. The collective "we" of a family of Kaqchikel speakers is further expanded into a collective group of Kaqchikels, marked in line by a reference to "our people" ("gente de nosotros" in line 59). This use of "our people" often acts to make it a gloss of the Kaqchikel term "qawinaq" and is a direct reference to a collective group of Kaqchikel speakers that stands in perceptual opposition to Ladi-nos and foreigners.

The ancient historical depth of Kaqchikel is another subtle recurring theme in the supplementary discourse of culture and its associated language ideologies. Another bilingual twenty-year-old maid living in Chi-maltenango, originally from the municipio of Tecpán, explained the following about Kaqchikel:

64) Kaqchikel es de un principio, es así.
    Kaqchikel is from the beginning, it's like that.

This young woman asserted that "Kaqchikel is from the beginning," sit-uating Kaqchikel at the beginning of time or at the beginning of the community. The history of Kaqchikel, along with its collective cultural heritage, is visible in the words of another bilingual woman who was thirty years old and working as a marketer. She assessed the importance of speaking Kaqchikel in the following way:

65) Es algo que viene desde el principio con mi cultura.
    It is something that comes from the beginning with my culture.
66) En segundo lugar que, es un privilegio de hablarlo.
    Secondly, it is a privilege to speak it.

Like the young maid mentioned above, this woman understood Kaqchikel as passed down to her and other speakers from "the beginning"—"es algo que viene desde el principio" (line 65). She explicitly associated Kaqchikel with the beginning of her culture, a culture she objectifies through personal possession in line 65.

The centrality of Mayan languages to ethnonationalist cultural revitalization is the third theme in the supplementary discourse of culture. Its presence is evidenced in explicit revitalization talk by roughly 25 percent of the people with whom we spoke. For example, a thirty-five-year-old Spanish monolingual market woman highlighted the newfound importance of Kaqchikel and other Mayan languages:

67) Mi papá quería que nosotros aprendiéramos bien el castellano
    My father wanted us to learn Spanish very well
68) porque así nos puede desenvolver mejor. Pero ahora me doy cuenta
    because with it we could develop ourselves better. But now I realize
69) que el kaqchikel es muy importante. Bueno, ahora pues, es muy
    that Kaqchikel is very important. Well, now it is very
70) importante aprender un idioma, cualquier idioma sea kaqchikel, el
    important to learn a language, whatever language, be it Kaqchikel,
71) k'iche', el q'eqchi' porque ahora están, como le diría,
    K'iche' or Q'eqchi', because now there are, how will I say it,
72) hay muchas instituciones que están promoviendo el kaqchikel, así como
    there are many institutions that are promoting Kaqchikel, like
73) las asociaciones mayas.
    the Mayan associations.

This Spanish monolingual woman remembered her father as the agent of language choices in the household. He wanted his children "to learn Spanish very well" (line 67), a desire that became a functional reality as evidenced in her discourse above, which does not show marked features of Spanish with Mayan influences. In this family, as in many others, learning Spanish was perceived to be necessarily at the expense of

Kaqchikel—the zero-sum equation that furthered the ideology of exclusivity that I discussed in chapter 1. While this market woman implies a past agreement with her father's choice, she goes on to contrast her earlier belief ("pero" in line 68) with the way she feels at present ("ahora" in line 69). She expresses a new consciousness ("me doy cuenta que el kaqchikel es muy importante" in 68–69) about the importance of Mayan languages. She articulates an understanding of the new significance of Mayan languages in terms of a Maya cultural distinctiveness, a cultural distinctiveness that supports and creates ethnolinguistic boundaries. She claims that it is important to learn any Mayan language—be it Kaqchikel, K'iche', or Q'eqchi' (lines 70–71)—thereby re-entextualizing Pan-Maya notions of ethnolinguistic identity that valorize equally all Mayan languages in Guatemala in service of a unified peoplehood. The marked new perception of the importance of Mayan languages is explicitly tied to the work done by Maya NGOs. As the monolingual marketer explains, "Now there are many institutions that are promoting Kaqchikel, like Maya associations" (lines 72–73).

A similar consciousness of the importance of Mayan languages and cultural revitalization efforts was echoed in the words of a forty-year-old bilingual Maya-Kaqchikel woman. Unlike many of the other respondents at the time of our research, she was a highly educated woman working as a professional at the private Rafael Landívar University. Like many of our interlocutors, she was originally from a municipio of Chimaltenango, Patzún, and had migrated to the department capital. She, too, discussed the importance of Mayan languages for Maya cultural revitalization in metalinguistic speech:

74) También se están trabajando, pero, para la recuperación del
    Also they are working themselves, but, for the recuperation of the
75) idioma. Pero sí hay muchas instituciones. Por ejemplo, la
    language. But, yes, there are many institutions. For example, the
76) Universidad Rafael Landívar está haciendo mucho en esta área
    Rafael Landívar University is doing a lot in this area
77) para (???) Ahora, claro se pierde mucho que para poder hacer un buen
    to. . . . Now, certainly a lot is lost, but to give it a good
78) adelante, de que como es nuestro idioma, pues. Estaba algo (1), pues,
    push ahead, because it is our language. It was something, well,

79) abandonado, y ahora que están retomando no se puede decir que sí
    abandoned, and now that they are reclaiming it you can't say that
80) está haciéndolo pues. Porque el idioma lleva la cultura, si queremos
    it is happening. Because the language carries the culture, and if we
81) ser personas realizadas tenemos que también tener
    want to be successful people, we have to also have
82) nuestra cultura, y el idioma es parte fundamental de la cultura.
    our culture, and the language is a fundamental part of the culture.

This bilingual professional Kaqchikel woman articulates the theme of Maya cultural revitalization in lines 74 and 75, explaining that there are many institutions working for the recuperation of Mayan languages. In addition to this explicit revitalization talk, she further articulates her own realization of the connection between Mayan languages and collective identity. Considering the connection between language and collective identity to be inextricable in the Whorfian frame promoted by Pan-Maya linguists, she explains that "the language carries the culture, and if we want to be successful people, we have to also have our culture, and language is a fundamental part of the culture" (lines 80–82). By locating culture in language, she invests Mayan languages with the agency of cultural transmission and distinction for Maya peoples. In this conceptualization, a return to Mayan languages is not understood as a return to the past, but rather is an integral part of contemporary modern life—the objectified culture that a unified Maya people possesses in a contemporary era. The metaphor of incremental advancement, the modernist ideal of linear progress par excellence, is explicitly applied to revitalization efforts, as "pushing" the language ahead ("para poder hacer un buen adelante," lines 77–78). In this woman's metalinguistic speech, possessing a distinct language is understood to be a unique object to "be scrutinized, displayed, and revitalized" (Handler 1988:12). It is an understanding that highlights the importance of collective Maya cultural difference in post-conflict Guatemala.

The supplementary discourse of culture coexisted with the discourse of progress in the practical consciousness of indigenous people with whom we spoke. At times, there was a personal identification with Maya institutions working to revitalize Mayan languages, even among bilingual speakers who self-consciously stopped speaking Mayan languages in their daily lives. For example, the forty-three-year-old bilingual man who elaborately articulated the "change of life" and change of language from Kaqchikel to Spanish as necessary outcomes of entering modernity (lines 27–51) animatedly discussed Pan-Maya revitalization efforts with me:

83) Entonces, ahora hay instituciones que están tratando, o ya
   So, now there are institutions that are trying, or already have
84) se trató de hacer directamente con todo los contextos de un silabario.
   tried to directly make a syllabary in all contexts.
85) Y tenemos ahora. Estas instituciones están ahora dando
   And now we have one. These institutions are now giving
86) clases a las niñas, a la gente netamente indígena, para, para, para
   classes to the girls, to the people who are truly indigenous, to, to, to
87) sobresalir. (1) Estoy enterando directamente por la prensa. La
   improve themselves. I'm finding out directly through the
88) prensa ahora está tirando de que todo que están interesado a
   press. The press now is putting out the word that anyone who is
89) perfeccionar su, su lenguaje, el kaqchikel. Entonces ellos pueden
   interested in perfecting, their, their language, Kaqchikel. Then they can
90) asistir a estos cursos (3). Ahora ya empezamos, o empezaron
   attend these courses. Now we have started, or they have started,
91) algunas instituciones donde dan enfoques, por ejemplo con la "k"
   some institutions where they give emphasis, for example, with the "k"
92) poniendo apóstrofes, ya poniendo eso para donde enfoque lo que es
   putting apostrophes, now putting that to show where the emphasis is
93) la palabra para, para modificar estas palabras.
   in the word to, to modify these words.

Although this man articulates the most comprehensive versions of the discourse of progress, he speaks passionately about Maya linguistic revitalization. He expresses awareness of and endorsement for the creation of grammatical materials (a syllabary in line 84), language classes for indigenous children (line 90), and writing systems for Mayan languages like Kaqchikel (lines 91–92). All of his points are, in fact, basic understandings of Maya language activists' notable achievements that were discussed in earlier chapters. While explicitly disassociating himself with speaking Kaqchikel and the entire way of life associated with it, this bilingual clerk simultaneously identifies with Maya cultural revitalization efforts. His ambivalence is illustrated in his shifting use of "we" in the transcript above. In line 85, he claims "we have" ("tenemos") a syllabary, meaning "we" speakers of Kaqchikel. He also includes himself in revitalization efforts like modifying the writing system of Kaqchikel to express its phonetics more adequately. He says "now we have started" (line 90) and then corrects himself, saying, "[some institutions] have started" in lines 90 and 91. His metalinguistic talk embodies the shifting identifications that happen as the discourse of progress is momentarily interrupted by the discourse of culture in the practical consciousness of some urban highland Kaqchikels.

Another bilingual man, who was working as a bookkeeper and who migrated from Tecpán to Chimaltenango, emphasized the new relevance of Mayan languages in direct relation to Guatemalan national politics. He remarked about the efforts to officialize Mayan languages:

94) Pues, la verdad es necesario. Yo pienso que deberían de hacerlo
    Well, the truth is it is necessary. I think that they should do
95) y posiblemente, con lo mucho que están haciendo como,
    it and maybe they will, with everything that they are doing like,
96) nos, ya, nos están dando un poco de (2) de (2) lugar asi en
    us, now, they are giving us a little bit of, of a place in
97) la política. . . . Considero que es un orgullo que
    politics. . . . I consider it an honor that
98) lo oficialicen.
    they may officialize it.

Again, the collective "we" of Maya peoples is invoked with talk of officializing Mayan languages in lines 96 and 97 when he explains, "they are giving us a little bit of a place in politics." Explicitly linking Mayan language revitalization with governmental democratization efforts, this man notes the political changes happening in Guatemala in the years immediately following the peace accords and situates revalorization of Mayan languages directly within it. In this man's consciousness, Mayan languages momentarily become assets, things one can be proud of (line 97) rather than things that must be disparaged in order to have material, economic, and social opportunities in the modern era.

In sum, collectively, these three themes—the familial continuity of Kaqchikel speakers, the deep historical presence and perseverance of the language, and explicit talk about Pan-Maya language revitalization efforts

—constitute a supplementary discourse of culture that disrupts the dominant discourse of progress and its associated language ideologies that promote and justify language shift from Kaqchikel to Spanish. By adding objectified "culture" as a significant aspect of life in the modern present, this cultural discourse disrupts the binary relational language ideologies that exclusively associate Kaqchikel with an undesirable way of life in the premodern past and associate Spanish with desirable ways of life in the modern present. In the discourse of culture, Kaqchikel weaves in and out of the discourse of progress as a valued object of and vehicle for an ethnolinguistic identity collectively shared in the ways that Maya scholars have propagated. Certainly, the extent of the impact of the discourse of culture and this impact's long-term implications are difficult to ascertain as changes, contradictions, and contestations continue to unfold.[13] Nevertheless, in this dynamic situation, Kaqchikel and Mayan languages are positively evaluated as part of a cultural, yet not essential, collective distinctiveness of Maya peoples in Guatemala.

The simultaneous production of both discourses—of progress and of culture—along with the ambivalence that such simultaneity creates, performs the ongoing contestation of language ideologies and their relationships to modernity and collective identity in late twentieth-century Guatemala. In this way, local ideologies of language among indigenous people from Chimaltenango support Bauman and Briggs's (2003) argument that modernist discourses are hegemonic when mapped onto language and identity. At the same time, local language ideologies reconfigure "modern" identity in ways that disrupt the totalizing effect of Bauman and Briggs's theoretical account. More specifically, the supplementary discourse of progress reconfigures "culture" expressed through language as a more inclusive, albeit circumscribed, part of modern indigenous identification. In contrast to nationalist language ideologies, the grassroots ideologies of language in the discourse of culture do not promote an essential relationship between language and identity. Indeed, the discourse of culture challenges the exclusive equation of Mayan languages with Maya ethnolinguistic identity, precisely because it situates Spanish as a fundamental part of one's identity as a modern person, a point that I take up in more detail in the following chapter. Far from essentializing identities based on the use or disuse of Mayan languages, the supplementary discourse of culture links Mayan speakers to a specific culture and a unique heritage as a unified people. By highlighting the importance of culture, it reconfigures Mayan languages as sites for forming cultural identities in the modern present. However, Kaqchikel is conceptualized more as an object of valor than as a practice of daily life.

CHAPTER 5

Traditional Maya Women and Linguistic Reproduction

PERHAPS THE MOST VISIBLE negotiation of modernity, language ideology, and collective identity in the bilingual Western highlands of Guatemala is refracted through the lens of gender, in particular, through representations of the "traditional" Maya woman. Representations of the "traditional" Maya woman, monolingual and brightly dressed, are ubiquitous in and out of Guatemala; they blanket postcards, travel brochures, academic book covers, and myriad other publicly circulating constructions of Mayaness (see fig. 5).

Such a regularly essentialized understanding of indigenous women's relationship to cultural tradition, not surprisingly, is recursively projected onto women's linguistic conservatism in a variety of discourses and contexts. In particular, the ideologically loaded construction of Maya women as the bearers of linguistic tradition is commonplace in both sociolinguistic and Pan-Maya scholarship. In the former, women are often taken to be linguistically conservative; in the latter, they are presumed to be monolingual speakers of Mayan languages who instrumentally reproduce future generations of native Mayan speakers. In both cases, women are conceptualized as "traditional" in tacit opposition to "modern" men in much the same way Bauman and Briggs's (2003) historical analysis has suggested; namely, they are situated as "traditional" Others within modern society in ways that tend to further their marginalization.

However, some young urban Maya women from the Chimaltenango area challenge this construction of the "traditional" Maya woman and her relationships to linguistic conservatism and social reproduction. Through an analysis of men's and women's differing linguistic identification, I aim to show how gendered experiences of linguistic tradition challenge the homogenizing assumptions of some sociolinguists and frustrate Pan-Maya political goals to reproduce an exclusive form of Mayaness among future

generations. These young, urban Maya women are challenging the unintended homogenizing effects of sociolinguistic scholarship that have
tended to essentialize indigenous women's agency, as well as the unanticipated tacit exclusion of monolingual Spanish speakers from the Maya
movement's ethnolinguistic project. In both instances, young Spanish-
monolingual-identified Maya women subvert Bauman and Briggs' (2003)
universalizing conception of the way in which women are neatly aligned
with tradition in the production of modernist language ideologies and
social inequalities. In fact, these young indigenous women identify as
agents of modernity rather than as bearers of tradition.

The Gender of Maya Tradition

As we have seen, the cornerstone of the Maya ethnolinguistic political
project is the essential link between Mayan languages and Maya peoplehood. To ensure that connection is imagined as inherent, the Pan-Maya
movement relies fundamentally on perceptions of Maya women as the
primary reproducers of "traditional" language upon which the politics of
collective unification rests. Such representations of women's instrumental position in cultural reproduction tend to be naturalized by Pan-Maya
leaders. Kay Warren explains: "For Mayas, women are powerful metonymic representations of community because they are felt to be central to
the continuity of Maya culture in their roles as bearers of the next generation and socializers of the children in Mayan languages" (1998:108).
Indeed, such representations of women's maintenance of tradition tend
to be naturalized by Pan-Maya leaders. Anthropologist Irma Otzoy un-
equivocally comments on those with whom she identifies: "Maya women
feel the strongest sense of cultural responsibility to transmit their values to
future generations" (1996:147). This gendered responsibility for the reproduction of "traditional" culture is often attributed to the intrinsic moral
strength of Maya women, a commonplace claim in Maya intellectual
circles, despite the role that men necessarily play in this process.[1]

While Maya women's instrumentality is elevated to a central role
in cultural maintenance, questions concerning gendered subjectivity
among Maya communities often go publicly unacknowledged within the
movement. In this way, the doxa of Nikte's recent proposal to rename
the language variety Achi as Rab'inalchii', discussed in chapter 3, is as

Figure 5. Publicly circulating gendered icons of Maya identity, as shown in oversized kite made for All Saint's Day festival in Sumpango, Guatemala (by author).

impressive as its intervention. As I mentioned, *achi* is a masculine term referring to man. Yet when Nikte' marshals a critique of the name "achi" to represent her native language, her position makes no mention of gender, despite the fact that the name functions as a generic masculine. The absence of any discussion of gender is particularly noteworthy (yet unmarked) in that Nikte' is one of a handful of senior Maya women scholars working within the Pan-Maya movement. Such masculine language used to name a mixed-gender referent, such as a language variety spoken by both men and women, is often ideologized as exclusionary in movements that call for more inclusive societies (Silverstein 1985). Nevertheless, there has tended to be a generalized silence about gender among Maya anthropologists and linguists involved in the movement who typically regard gender as a divisive issue and questions about gender as undermining the project of Pan-Maya unification (Nelson 1999). For example, in an interview with anthropologist Diane Nelson (1999), Dr. Demetrio Cojtí criticized Maya women who would push for a serious discussion of gender: "They are separatists! They can't have a separate space—don't they realize they are half of the Maya movement? They are dividing us" (168).

While Pan-Maya assumptions about women's linguistic tradition and role in social reproduction tend to go unquestioned in public discourse, the Maya movement's reliance on that tradition for the political project of language revitalization adds another dimension to Bauman and Briggs's understanding of the relationship between tradition and linguistic ideologies. Bauman and Briggs suggest that the identification of women with linguistic tradition is a means for creating premodern Others who are subordinated within a hierarchical social order (2003:14). Certainly, the ubiquitous representation of "traditional" Maya women in a national context where indigenous women are the poorest and most illiterate members of society lends support to Bauman and Briggs's theory. At the same time, this perceived relationship between Maya women and linguistic tradition is the basis upon which collective Maya selves are made among future generations. It will be these new generations who, ideally, will be included politically, economically, and culturally as equals in the Guatemalan nation. In the Guatemalan case, the women's "traditional" identities are vehicles by which modern inclusions become imaginable for Maya ethnonationalism.

Sociolinguistic Representations of
Linguistic Conservatism

This explicit orientation toward women as instruments of cultural reproduction is also assumed in a large body of sociolinguistic scholarship on language contact and variation spanning two decades of research,
from the early 1970s to the early 1990s. Generally supporting specific
ethnonationalist assumptions about Maya women as "traditional," North
American sociolinguistic scholarship has frequently situated women un-
problematically as metonymic reproducers of culture and its central constituent, language. Indeed, representations of women's strong ties to "traditional" aspects of cultural identity, particularly native languages, abound
in sociolingusitic research. Frequently, research has argued that women
are more linguistically conservative than men in language contact situations (Farber 1978; Hill 1987; Kulick 1992). This means that women are
reported to remain steadfastly monolingual in local languages, while men
more quickly acquire access to and use of dominant/colonizing languages,
often at the loss of their native language. In these instances, the gendering
of linguistic tradition centers on the women of the community, who are
presumed to keep local languages alive and pass them on to their children,
thereby producing future native speakers. This general trend of thought in
cross-cultural sociolinguistic scholarship done in the 1970s through the
early 1990s has guided the prevailing orientation toward Maya women's
linguistic conservatism in Western highland Maya communities in Guatemala (Farber 1978; Smith 1996; Fischer 1996; Richards 1998).[2]

Sociolinguists writing with this orientation are quick to note that the
marked exception to the trend of linguistic traditionalism among women
concerns situations in which the shift from local to dominant languages
advances to the final stages of the process, resulting in language shift. In
these instances, women reportedly move from linguistic "conservatism"
to linguistic "innovation," moving rapidly and en masse toward language
shift, while men in their communities continue to maintain the local
language as bilinguals (Gal 1984; Hill 1987; Aikio 1992; Garzon 1998a).
Jane Hill explains this seemingly contradictory process involving women,
conservatism, and language shift situations in the following way: "In
studies of the role of women in language change conducted among speakers of world languages in urban centers, a paradoxical pattern has been

identified. . . . Women are more conservative than men in cases of stable variation, but are more innovative in cases of change in progress, particularly if the change is assimilation toward an elite norm" (1987:121). From Hill's analytic perspective, as in many recent interventions into language and gender research, scholars have rightly complicated essentialized understandings of women's relation to linguistic tradition (Brody 1991; Eckert and McConnell-Ginet 1992; Brown 1993; Bucholtz 2003). Regarding the specific case of urban bilingual women in language contact situations who shift toward the dominant language, Hill readily characterizes these women's code choices as "innovative." Nevertheless, with an eye toward the assumptions of sociolinguists and linguistic anthropologists as ideologically loaded, I want to highlight that the act of rendering a gendered linguistic phenomenon "paradoxical" becomes possible only when analysts take for granted the innately "traditional" nature of women. From this common scholarly perspective, the unmarked social fact is women's "traditional" language use. The marked exception to that fact is women's change toward linguistic "innovation" in the final stages of language shift. Within this framework, it follows that women taking up the hegemonic/outside code can be explained only as a sudden and aberrant switch to "innovative" linguistic behavior when women tacitly fail to reproduce traditional language practices in expected ways.

Sociolinguist Marjut Aikio elaborates upon scholarly understandings of the perceptual paradox surrounding women's "traditional" and "innovative" uses of language in multilingual contact situations:

> On the one hand it is claimed that women are more traditional than men in their linguistic behavior and that they learn a second language (L2) to a lesser extent than men do. This had been explained through women's lesser mobility. On the other hand, the claim is made that women are greater innovators than men and that they learn the standard language more quickly; the argument is that because of their weaker economic position, generally inferior status vis a vis men, and, in particular, the increase in duties in the service sector requiring verbal communication, women must adopt behaviors (including linguistic ones) which contribute to upward mobility in the social hierarchy. (1992:43)

While Aikio continues to uphold the logic of "paradox" in women's switch from linguistic conservation to linguistic innovation, she does direct scholarly attention to considerations of social mobility, economic status, and power in order to explain women's linguistic behaviors relative to their instrumental use of codes. In this way, Aikio calls for expanding our understanding of the "paradox" from exclusively gendered terms to a more multifaceted account.

Renowned sociolinguist William Labov tackles this paradoxical problem more directly from an economic angle, suggesting that the shift from women's linguistic conservatism to linguistic "innovation" is definitively tied to economic factors. Labov argues that "shifts from one language to another are inevitably conscious and are always changes from above . . . such shifts, like the dialect redistributions, are often tightly tied to economic factors" (1990:214). While Labov underscores the effects of economic motivations implicated in the paradox of women's language use, he clearly attributes the agency for such a shift as one imposed from the outside, rather than chosen from the inside, by women. To make this argument, Labov relies on a stereotypical notion of women's feminine weakness and vulnerability as warranting these imposed effects of language change upon them. Within this frame, women's paradoxical and final innovation in language-shift situations is thereby understood by the analyst to be "essentially the adoption of a norm external to the speech community, and groups with high linguistic insecurity are most sensitive to such norms" (1990:213). Labov identifies the reason that women succumb to external economic and social forces as their high level of insecurity, thereby implying that if women were secure and confident, they wouldn't betray their communities' local linguistic norms in favor of external ones. In other words, Labov blames women for failed social reproduction even as he denies their agency in the process.

These varied linguistic ideological assumptions implicit in scholarly constructions of the "paradox" of women's linguistic conservatism and final innovative shift, on the one hand, and Pan-Maya assumptions about women's "natural" propensity to transmit indigenous language to future generations, on the other, converge in a significant way. Both scholars' and activists' perspectives on language shift and gender assume and, indeed, circumscribe women's subject positions as fundamentally grounded in "tradition" and fixed as social actors. When women are "paradoxically" innovative, as several prominent scholars of language claim, the suddenness presumed in the shift from one language to another is one only of *position* in an essentialist understanding of women's identity relative to language. Women are either the instrumental bearers or the instrumental abandoners of local languages—that is to say, of tradition. In other words, from the sociolinguistic and Pan-Maya perspectives outlined above, women are reified in instances of language contact as *vehicles* of change rather than *agents* of it.

As we will see, the multivalent ideological association of Maya women with the social reproduction of traditional language is another essential construct that local experiences of language and identity challenge. While this may or may not be evident in other highland communities, it is particularly prevalent in the urban environs of Chimaltenango that I discussed in the previous chapter. Young urban Maya women living in the highland city of Chimaltenango are identifying as Spanish monolinguals, an identification based on local experiences of tradition and the disciplining of it through language. As I will argue, these women's ideologies of language situate them as agents rather than mere vehicles of modernity. They thereby challenge pervasive assumptions about women's instrumentality in linguistic and social reproduction. Before presenting the data upon which I make this claim, I turn to briefly discuss the relationship between language biographies and the process of identification in order to more fully consider how young urban Maya women choose to represent themselves in public discourse like the sociolinguistic interviews Miriam and I conducted.

Women and Linguistic Identification

Variationist sociolinguistics tends to rely on quantitative correlations between linguistic features and social categories to make claims about significant relationships. However, such data may be even more useful to language analysts if they are reconceptualized from solely "objective facts" to also "subjective performances" rich in revealing processes of *identification*. For our consideration of women's linguistic choices, tradition, and forms of identity in urban highland Guatemala, redirecting attention toward individual and collective identification may enhance the study of women's roles as agents in language change in a "modern" era. As we have seen, a good deal of research concerned with language shift, both in and out of Guatemala, has relied heavily upon a sociolinguistic paradigm that draws upon quantitative methodologies to evaluate the rate and degree of shift from one language to another (Weinreich 1968; Fishman 1972; Dorian 1981, 1989; Gal 1979, 1984; Powell 1989; Labov 1990; Richards and Richards 1990; Brown 1991; Garzon 1991; Fischer 1996). This work often assesses language shift by collecting language surveys, censuses, and language bibliographies among sample populations. These kinds of data enable researchers to correlate specific social variables like gender, age, class, ethnicity, and the like with degrees of language shift. Sociolinguist Fernando Peñalosa, who has worked extensively with Mayan languages, explains this orientation in *Introduction to the Sociology of Language*: "[W]e predict that under certain stated conditions, the presence of certain variables (quantified, if possible) will produce given results. For example, if the theory states that certain linguistic phenomena are to be explained by certain social configurations or processes, then whenever we find the latter, we should expect to find the same linguistic phenomena" (1981:10). While these quantitative data are useful in correlating social factors with language shift, I propose that they may yield less information about objective numbers of speakers and degrees of language loss and more information about collective identifications at work among a given group. In other words, such quantitative correlations between language features and social variables tend to "rationalize, systemize, and naturalize a sociolinguistic schema that explains the indexical relationships as autonomous of the indexical phenomena to be understood" (Silverstein 1998:129). Silverstein's attention to the ideological aspects of correlation means that individuals' self-reporting of language abilities elicited in the study of language shift may be productively reframed as constituting, in given contexts where metalinguistic ideologies are brought to the fore, individuals' social identifications. By this I mean, "the ways in which ideas about our personal identity are formed by spontaneously, intuitively, and sometimes unconsciously identifying with others and institutions such as family, nation, political or cultural cause" (Burke 1966:301). How individuals report their language ability is inextricably connected with how they understand their social identity—the social groups with which they identify and how they hope others will perceive them. A focus on identification enables me to highlight the ideological aspects of language shift embedded in the data generated by sociolinguistic studies that are centered on deriving correlations from quantifiable variables.

To show how some urban Kaqchikel women's identifying practices challenge the essential construct of women as instruments of linguistic tradition, I turn to discuss quantitative data from the sociolinguistic survey discussed in the previous chapter. Overall, the majority of people identified as speakers of Spanish and a Mayan language (predominantly Kaqchikel). Sixty-four percent (eighty-two individuals) reported that they spoke Spanish and a Mayan language, either Kaqchikel, K'iche', or Q'eqchi'. Nevertheless, 36 percent of the respondents (forty-six people) reported that they were monolingual in Spanish (see figs. 6 and 7). This sample population indicates that Mayan languages are still socially significant languages in the Chimaltenango area. Yet the respondents also show a definite transition toward and an explicit preference for identification as Spanish monolinguals.[3]

For our consideration of women's relation to linguistic tradition and social reproduction, it is important to understand how saliently, in this study, gender correlated with identification as a Spanish monolingual speaker.[4] Fifty-four percent of women in the survey (forty-one women) reported that they spoke both Spanish and a Mayan language; 46 percent (thirty-five women) reported that they spoke only Spanish. This trend contrasts with men; 78 percent (forty) of the men reported that they spoke both Spanish and a Mayan language. Few men, only 22 percent (twelve), identified themselves as Spanish monolinguals. Clearly, there is a much higher level of self-reported monolingualism in Spanish among urban Maya women than among Maya men in this study (see figs. 8 and 9).

Looking more specifically at the younger segment of the group further supports that there is a significant trend toward an explicit preference for identifying as an exclusive Spanish speaker among Maya women. Among women ages thirteen to thirty-nine (forty-eight women), 62.5 percent (thirty individuals) claimed to be monolingual Spanish speakers. For men in the same age group (thirty-three individuals), only 27.3 percent (nine) self-identified in language biographies as Spanish monolinguals.

While generally eschewing identification as "traditional" Kaqchikel speakers, the young women surveyed wore markedly indigenous clothing and claimed indigenous family. In short, they identified themselves as

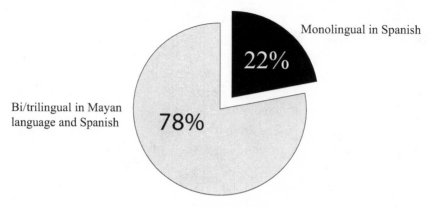

Figure 6. Men's linguistic identification (by Sondi Burnell).

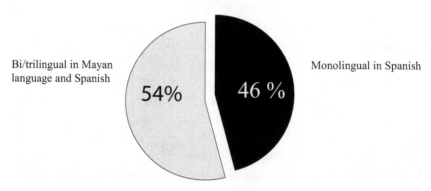

Figure 7. Women's linguistics identification (by Sondi Burnell).

indigenous and represented themselves publicly as Maya, even though frequently not as speakers of Mayan languages. Their dual identification as indigenous women and as Spanish monolinguals underscores alternative linguistic ideologies connecting tradition with identity in nonessentialist ways, at least among this select group of young urban Maya women. These dual identifications as indigenous and as exclusive Spanish speakers challenge Pan-Maya assumptions about women's inherent reproduction of "traditional" Mayan languages, as well as tacit sociolinguistic assumptions about women's mere instrumentality in language change processes.

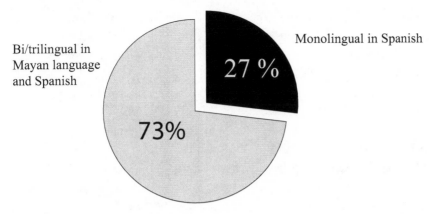

Figure 8. Linguistic identification of men ages 12–39 (by Sondi Burnell).

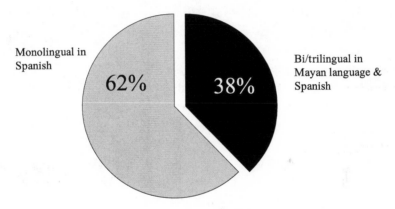

Figure 9. Linguistic identification of women ages 12–39 (by Sondi Burnell).

In the context of multiethnic public life in Chimaltenango at the end of the twentieth century, women's dual identification as Mayas and as Spanish monolinguals seemed to be unproblematic for this select group. Such identifications indicate how urban Maya women's identity is constituted by several different identifications and concomitant ideologies. Two are particularly important for our consideration of the role of women in linguistic and social reproduction. The first is a locally held understanding of tradition based upon a recent history of women's experiences.

The second is the manner in which notions of tradition become mapped onto language codes. We must attend to the ways that the two become linked. I argue that the reason why women are more likely than men to identify as Spanish monolinguals is tied to gendered experiences of tradition and to the articulation of those experiences with the locally spoken Mayan language, Kaqchikel.

In her discussion of tradition, gender roles, and collective Maya identity in Guatemala, cultural anthropologist Carol Smith (1996) explains that the disciplining of Maya women's daily lives was one of the central components of postcolonial gender politics in local highland communities: "In the 1970s the Maya, like all other Guatemalans, accepted an essentialist construct as the basis of ethnic identity. Identity was community specific, based upon an extremely high rate of endogamy. . . . The maintenance of Maya women's parochialism (through dress and language) helped to maintain Maya women as marital partners for Maya men, in community-specific ways" (63–64). As a result of women's parochialism and community endogamous marriage patterns, Smith argues, "Maya women exchanged the freedom to abandon their communities for personal security within their communities so long as they avoided contact with men from outside the area" (1996:65). Here, Smith underscores the ways in which gender was disciplined through local understandings of "tradition" during a recent modern era in highland Maya communities. Women remained tied to local tradition through the public maintenance of culture in such a way that it concomitantly provided them a measure of protection within the community that poor Ladino women did not have. What Smith overlooks in her analysis is the centrality of *language* in this process of disciplining women to facilitate the social reproduction of local indigenous identity.

A careful reconsideration of sociolinguistic research done in the Chimaltenango department indicates that the regimentation of women's linguistic codes (Spanish and Kaqchikel) became a key mechanism for maintaining the general practices Smith (1996) describes. In fact, during the pre-Violence era, social pressure to conform to highland Maya communities' gender expectations assumed the form of social sanctions against Maya women who violated local tradition by learning Spanish (Farber 1978; Smith 1996). Farber's research in the Comalapa municipio of the Chimaltenango department found that women's employment was commonly restricted to the home and/or local community, where Kaqchikel was spoken with "insiders." The only women who self-identified as Spanish speakers were women who had jobs that required them to travel and interact with Indians and Ladinos outside the local community. These women, having violated the expectations of local tradition by publicly speaking Spanish, were suspected of being dishonest, neglecting their children, and being unfaithful to their husbands (Farber 1978:250). In other words, these women were disciplined in the community because they did not fulfill their expected roles as instruments of linguistic tradition and social reproduction.

These kinds of sanctions against women's use of Spanish also happened in other Kaqchikel communities. For example, in the neighboring municipio of San Martín, only young women employed as maids in Guatemala City self-identified as Spanish speakers (Powell 1989:54).[5] This identification defied locally prescribed gender parochialism and linked directly to economic opportunities outside the community. During the same pre-genocidal era, the gendered maintenance of linguistic tradition was further promoted by many indigenous families that frequently kept young Maya girls out of formal education in Spanish (Farber 1978; Nelson 1999). In short, Maya women were often obliged to speak only Kaqchikel and were frequently denied access to economic and educational possibilities available through Spanish. These practices were done in the name of upholding local "tradition" that served to promote community endogamy and identity. When women identified with Spanish, and thus worked outside the community or studied through formal education, they transgressed normative gender roles.

Women's transgressive practices in education and labor that began during the Violence (Farber 1978; Garzon 1998b) increased during the post-Violence era as displacement from natal indigenous communities grew. Young urban women's gendered understandings of language and identity may work against maintaining linguistic tradition that was historically used to marginalize them within their own communities. In other words, some young urban Maya women living in Chimaltenango rejected local understandings of tradition that were disciplined through the preferred use of Kaqchikel and the restriction of Spanish for their mothers' and grandmothers' generations. Consequently, these young urban Maya women embraced what they conceived of as "modern" language practices. As I demonstrated in the previous chapter, in local metalinguistic discourse, Kaqchikel is indexically linked with themes of parochialism; a lack of education; rural, isolated living; and the hardship of poverty. Conversely, Spanish is the signifier of "modern" life with perceived increased educational opportunities, cosmopolitanism, migration, and economic advancement; this is the explicitly named "modern" moment that these Chimaltecas perceive to be attainable. These women, significantly more than their male counterparts, define themselves as Spanish monolinguals because of the perceived increased access to education and cash-earning labor activities. These perceived benefits, are, in turn, key aspects of modernity that were particularly more inaccessible to women than to men in Kaqchikel communities a generation ago (Smith 1996). Thus, urban Maya women's new identification as indigenous Spanish monolinguals indicates how axes of identification have transformed such that modernity (vis-à-vis Spanish) and Maya identity (self-identification) may obtain together in nonessentialist ways. As such, these women are meaning-making agents of social change rather than mere instruments of social reproduction.

While Maya scholars and activists readily assume women will reproduce linguistic tradition in service of future generations of collective Maya-speaking selves, it may very well be that women's increasing identification as Spanish monolinguals offers one of the greatest challenges to the tacit exclusions of their movement. Young Spanish-monolingual-identified Maya women in the Chimaltenango area challenge Pan-Maya politics to address the perspectives of indigenous, nonnative speakers of Mayan languages and to consider publicly the role of gender in their progressive moment. In other words, young indigenous women's identification as Spanish monolinguals obliges the Maya movement to become more inclusive of nonethnolinguistically bound definitions of contemporary indigenous identity. These same women's identifications concomitantly challenge sociolinguistic ideologies that presuppose that women are the most conservative speakers and mere instrumental reproducers of native languages in multilingual language contact situations. Taken together, young urban Maya women's position as agents of modernity disrupt Bauman and Briggs's (2003) theoretical account of the uniform manner in which women are exclusively linked with tradition. In this ethnographic instance, young indigenous women are unabashedly modern.

CHAPTER 6

Conclusion
*Vernacular Modernities and the
Objectification of Tradition*

HAVING TRAVERSED SOME ethnographic and social terrain of language
ideologies circulating in the bilingual indigenous highlands of Guatemala, I want to return circuitously to Bauman and Briggs's theoretical inquiry into modernity and inequality. Bauman and Briggs propose that the
"traditional" and the "modern" are relationally constructed and mapped
onto ideologies of language. I suggest that at the end of the twentieth century, modernity—rather than ethnolinguistic identity—was the key trope
of cultural politics in urban bilingual Guatemala to be negotiated, challenged, and reconfigured by the Maya movement and its interlocutors.

As we have seen throughout the book, the Guatemalan state, local
bilingual Maya communities in the Kaqchikel and K'iche' regions, and
language analysts are all invested in modern political formations (nationalism), epistemologies (linguistic science), and negotiations of "modern" personhood. Thus, Bauman and Briggs's (2003) theoretical account
of the manner in which modernity and language ideologies are implicated in structuring social exclusions is empirically demonstrated in the
case of late twentieth-century Guatemala. More specifically, hegemonic
state discourses and practices of nation building have excluded Maya
peoples from the nation, local knowledge has been marginalized by the
authority of linguistic science, and Spanish-monolingual-identified indigenous women have been tacitly excluded from belonging to a collective
Maya-ethnolinguistic group because they do not fulfill their expected role
in social reproduction.

The very concept of the modern nation-state and its legitimacy as a
political and cultural unit have become so naturalized that oftentimes, a
nation's ability to craft a homogenous collective identity is a measure of its
success in the modern world (Gellner 1983; Handler 1988; Anderson

1991). As I discussed in chapter 1, it was within the institutional development of a national homogenizing project that Maya cultural and linguistic difference became a political, social, and economic "problem" to be
overcome by the state and its agents. In the Guatemalan case, national
"progress" within an explicitly modernist frame was the basis upon which
highland Maya communities were forced to experience horrific state-
sponsored violence that included compulsory assimilation, military con-
scription, obligatory adult literacy classes at the threat of death, and murder. These acts of violence in service of eradicating Maya distinctiveness
within the Guatemalan nation are underscored in Don Fidencio's memories, in Nikte's formal education, and in indigenous genocide survivors'
testimonies (CEH 1999; Sanford 2003).

While modernity has framed the state's homogenizing and violent
policies toward Maya peoples, another refraction of modernity has been
central to the Maya movement's creative challenge to the national politics of linguistic and cultural exclusion. As I illustrated in chapters 1 and 2,
Maya scholars and activists have used and, indeed, privileged the epistemology of science to justify and valorize the importance of Mayan linguistic difference. For Maya scholars and activists, scientific criteria and
rational linguistics are the legitimized means to analytically describe,
represent, and promote Mayan languages in response to the exclusionary
efforts of the state. The analysis of Mayan languages, in turn, provides
the basis upon which Maya scholars "objectively" define ethnolinguistic
communities, which are questionably meaningful at local levels, in service of cultural rights claims upon the Guatemalan nation and the international community. It is upon this scaffolding of modernity that the
Maya ethnolinguistic politics of cultural autonomy rests.

Nevertheless, even as scientific epistemology has been a productive
tool that Maya scholars have used to further their own political project of
Pan-Maya ethnolinguistic unification, it simultaneously legitimizes one
particular kind of knowledge—the knowledge of formally trained language analysts—at the potential expense of other ways of knowing. Such
expert knowledge may exclude alternative locally held understandings
of identity and language based upon history (as in the case of the Achis)
and gendered experiences of tradition (as in the case of young Spanish-
monolingual-identified indigenous women from the Chimaltenango de-

partment). In this way, tensions between the strategic essentialism of the Maya ethnolinguistic project and local bilingual Maya communities' experiences of language and identity indeed support Bauman and Briggs' argument that "critical social projects can, in fact, bolster key aspects of modernity they seek to challenge" (2003:309). In other words, my analysis of some language ideologies in post-conflict Guatemala suggests that as Pan-Maya scholars and activists seek to create a more inclusive Guatemalan nation for indigenous people, they may well create further exclusions of the majority Maya population. As I have begun to elucidate in this study, several Maya groups do not "fit" within the essential construction of ethnolinguistic identity in that they configure the language and identity relationship in other terms and, consequently, are not yet directly involved in the progressive Maya ethnolinguistic project.

Just as the nation-state and Pan-Maya movement deploy aspects of modernity in their political struggles, individual social actors in bilingual Kaqchikel and K'iche' communities foreground the importance of modernity and tradition relative to language and identity in their daily lives. Chapter 4 demonstrated how Chimaltecos' local ideologies of language link Spanish with the "the modern" and Kaqchikel with tradition in their metalinguistic discourse. In the Chimaltenango municipio, Spanish became the naturalized, ubiquitous code that one used to "get ahead" in the "modern" world through education and wage-labor economic advancement by the end of the twentieth century.

This increasingly common ideology of language found in metalinguistic discourse is also apparent in linguistic practice among some urban bilingual K'iche' communities. One example is evident in Choi's (2003) recent research among bilingual K'iche's from the urban center of Momostenango in the Totonicapán department. One of her consultants, Alfonso, a merchant living in the town center, recounted the following narrative about the limited opportunity for formal education and social advancement that his father's generation experienced:

1) Mi papá no estudió después de cinco años porque el papá de él
   My father didn't study after five years because his father
2) no quiso. Para él, no vale la pena. Él siempre preguntaba mi
   didn't want him to. For him, it wasn't worth it. He always asked my

3) papá, dice, "Ya katkuin tz'ib'anik?" Y mi papá decía,
   dad, saying, "Can you write yet?" And my father would say,
4) "Man kinkoin ta na." Entonces él podía continuar estudiando.
   "I don't know how to write yet." So he was able to continue studying.
5) Él era inteligente. Para estudiar más, él mentió.
   He was smart. To study more, he lied [to his father]. (2003:108)

Alfonso's narrative harkens back to a bygone time when formal education in Spanish was not a normative part of a young indigenous man's life because "it wasn't worth it" in terms of relative social prospects in a racist society that structurally excluded native peoples. The organic use of K'iche' in Alfonso's narrative iconically represents the past—literally the voice of Alfonso's grandfather, who questioned the utility of a Spanish education for his son, who would have limited economic opportunities outside his local community. The difficult and undesirable past is literally and metaphorically "revoiced" through the use of K'iche' in lines 3 and 4, with "Ya katkuin tz'ib'anik?" and "Man kinkoin ta na" (Choi 2003). In this way, local experiences of language and identity reconfigure a notion of Mayaness, possible through the use of Spanish based upon "modern" identifications that enable indigenous people to participate in economic and educational opportunities more available in urban areas than in rural areas, and more available at the end of the twentieth century than ever before.

At the same time, the indexical value of Kaqchikel and K'iche' as quintessential markers of Maya culture have recently been elevated due to Pan-Maya political efforts in the last two decades of the twentieth century. This means that, even as the use of Kaqchikel and K'iche' decreases for economic reasons, the languages' value as markers of Maya difference simultaneously increases for political reasons. A grassroots Kaqchikel literacy project in Comalapa, a *municipio* in the Chimaltenango department discussed in chapter 5, provides a telling example of this irony. After local leaders had worked with the Proyecto Lingüístico Francisco Marroquín (PLFM) and had become literate in Kaqchikel, they began literacy classes in their own community during the mid-1980s. Brown explains, "For three years about thirty-five adults, mostly under forty years of age, voluntarily attended night classes once a week for about two months" (1998:162). A decade later, local Kaqchikel-Mayas who participated in the class reflected upon the significance of the project. One Comalapense recalled: "After classes, we would leave, all of us speaking Kaqchikel" (Brown 1998:164). The literacy class momentarily encouraged a new use of and revealed a new value of Kaqchikel for the small group of adults who participated. But the quoted participant's following reflection reveals a more complicated, tacitly ambivalent ideology of language at play among the members of the class. He continued, "And to this day, we still greet each other in Kaqchikel" (Brown 1998:164). While Brown uses this example to celebrate the success of the literacy class for Kaqchikel revitalization (1998:164), I submit that participants' reflections on the class actually reveal the doxa of Spanish hegemony. By this I mean that Spanish remained firmly intact as the preferred code of use, even as the literacy class participants continued to "greet each other in Kaqchikel," indexically marking their collective identification as Maya. Implicitly, we come to understand that the remainder of their quotidian interactions following the greeting is conducted in the unmarked language, Spanish. Like those from the *cabecera* ("department seat") of Chimaltenango discussed in chapter 4, members of the San Juan Comalapa literacy class objectify Kaqchikel as a valued embodiment of Maya culture even as they recreate the hegemony of Spanish in their daily language use. Paradoxically, then, Kaqchikel becomes marked and valued ideologically even as Spanish comes to replace it in the practices of everyday life. This simultaneous distancing from and valorizing of Kaqchikel reveals an emerging, contradictory position of Mayan languages in the late modernity of post-conflict Guatemala among bilingual urban highland Kaqchikel and K'iche' communities.

The further significance of modernity for urban highland Kaqchikel Maya women's linguistic identification was borne out in chapter 5. Sociolinguistic data showed that young indigenous women, significantly more than men, identify as Spanish monolinguals in the Chimaltenango municipality. I argued that young women's keen identification as modern Spanish monolingual indigenous women is, in turn, tied to the gendering of cultural and linguistic "tradition" in particular ways. Women's Spanish use was sanctioned against among previous generations as part of local gender politics in highland indigenous communities during the mid-twentieth century. This disciplining of women's Spanish use has further disadvantaged their access to education and wage-labor activities outside the community in highland Kaqchikel and K'iche' areas (Menchú 1983; Powell 1989).[1]

Despite the omnipresence of concerns with "the modern" in a global context (Knauft 2002), as well as in bilingual highland Guatemalan indigenous communities, the manifestations and lived experiences of modernity are quite heterogeneous. In fact, such ethnographic diversity has led anthropologists and other scholars to challenge the very notion of a singular modernity. Instead of accepting this notion, they argue that a more accurate and rigorous analytic frame lies in a conception of multiple, vernacular modernities (Gaonkar 1999; Eisenstadt 2001; Knauft 2002). Hinton elaborates upon this perspective: "Modernity is a process that generates a variety of local forms. . . . 'Traditional others' are not passive recipients of modernity, but active meaning-making agents who, while operating within a set of structural constraints, nevertheless localize the global flow of ideas, technologies, and material goods associated with the modern world" (2002:8). It is the locally particular engagement with modernity (its political organization), the nation, and its economic system (late capitalism and its ideologies, consumption and progress) that are refracted in particular instantiations of "the modern" around the globe (Knauft 2002). In this way, modernities become multiple and heterogeneous.

These modernities become significant when they are productively juxtaposed with traditions (Errington and Gewertz 1996; Knauft 2002; Bauman and Briggs 2003). Heterogeneous understandings of "the modern" and "the traditional," as they are constituted through ideologies of language in some urban highland Guatemalan communities, allow us to redirect Bauman and Briggs's (2003) theoretical account into language ideologies, modernity, and inequality. Bauman and Briggs highlight how particular conceptions of language become a means by which "modern" identities are claimed in ways that serve to exclude various social groups. From their perspective, those who are excluded are those whose language embodies the "traditional." Hence, the "modern" is ideologically privileged and the "traditional" is used as a structuring device for marginalizing Others and perpetuating inequality.

However, the various examples from bilingual urban Kaqchikel and K'iche' communities discussed in this study allow scholars to see how "modernity" and "tradition" in fact *do not occupy fixed positions in the*

structuring of social exclusions and inclusions. On the contrary, local tradition refracted through historical and gendered consciousness of some
Maya citizens from Kaqchikel and K'iche' ethnolinguistic regions challenges the distinctly modern progressive Maya movement to be more
inclusive than it has been. When it does, notions of tradition are mobilized in service of more inclusive social efforts on behalf of Maya peoples
who do not identify with an essentialized understanding of language and
identity, such as the Achi community and young Spanish monolingual-
identified indigenous women. Thus, the multiplicity of modernities circulating in Guatemala and their diverse relationships to "tradition" challenge Bauman and Briggs's theoretical model to account for dynamism
and diversity at the ethnographic level.

Transnational Objectifications of Tradition

The strategic objectification of "tradition" is one of the key features of
vernacular modernities in a variety of Guatemalan contexts, a few of
which I have outlined in this book. In conclusion, I would like to suggest
that it may become equally important to the study of language ideologies,
inequality, and identity to consider objectifications of "tradition" of and
by Maya peoples in increasingly *transnational* contexts. Three sites may
be particularly significant for future critical ethnographic investigation,
including a tourism industry directed at North Americans and Western
Europeans, international development efforts to represent and discipline
"multiculturalism" in Guatemala, and immigration and human rights
issues involving Maya peoples in the United States. I will address each of
these briefly below.

Some bilingual Kaqchikel Maya vendors involved in international
tourism from the community of San Antonio Aguas Calientes provide a
compelling example of the strategic objectification of tradition. Little's
(2004) recent ethnography demonstrates how Antoneros families self-
consciously perform "traditional" Maya culture for North American and
European tourists. Members of the Lopez family—who speak Spanish
fluently; live in a house built of concrete; and have electricity, stoves, and
refrigerators—efficiently transform their house into a "traditional" Maya
dwelling. They convert their living space into a "theater-in-the-round that
involves partitioning off private areas of the house and removing electrical

appliances and other signs of non-Maya material culture" (2004:213). The family then borrows selectively from essentialized versions of "traditional" Maya culture during their staged performances of the "typical Indian life" in western highland Guatemala. For example, tourists are directed through the old section of the house with cane walls and dirt floors. Next, they are greeted by the Lopez women in full traditional dress, surrounded by *tipica* weavings, and hear Kaqchikel spoken amongst the members of the family (Little 2004:214–216).

The women's practices underscore the place of language ideologies in structuring self-conscious uses of tradition among bilingual urban Mayas. Enacting the very stereotype of the "traditional Maya woman" that I problematized in chapter 5, women from the Lopez family implore their foreign visitors, "Please excuse my poor Spanish. If I speak slowly, it is because Spanish is my second language, and it is difficult for me to find the correct words" (Little 2004:216–217). The irony is that the women are completely versed and literate in Spanish and conduct most public discourse in the language (Little 2004:217). In this way, language ideologies that link Kaqchikel with tradition in gendered ways are strategically mobilized for economic advancement in highly marked circumstances that involve the transnational circulation of peoples, commodities, and discourses.

International development efforts are increasingly involved in and committed to promoting very specific notions of multiculturalism in Guatemala. Not surprisingly, these efforts strategically objectify "traditional" aspects of Maya culture, such as Mayan languages. A 1998 edition of *Worldview*, the official publication of the United States Peace Corps Association, provides a telling example. The cover boldly announces: "New Governors: Guatemalan politics is now spoken in Quiche and Cakchiquel."[2] The cover juxtaposes these two large Mayan language names with the image of Rigoberto Quemé, the first indigenous mayor of Quetzaltenango, clad in Western clothing and claiming a central space within a colonial Spanish building. The accompanying article highlights Maya cultural activism and the emergent Maya "political class" in Guatemala (Karp 1998).

While international development agencies like the Peace Corps are quick to underscore the laudatory efforts of Maya cultural rights politics in post-conflict Guatemala, analysts must be careful to examine their limits. Hale's (2002) recent work suggests that the libratory promise of cultural rights activism may actually work in favor of neoliberal political and economic policies. Hale argues that "proponents of the neoliberal doctrine pro-actively endorse a substantive, if limited, version of indigenous cultural rights, as a means to resolve their own problems and advance their own political agendas" (2002:487). His work highlights the notion that transnational institutions like the World Bank and USAID recognize Maya culture and endorse multicultural ideals, even as these are "precautionary and pre-emptive reforms, actions taken to cede carefully chosen ground in order to more effectively fend off more far-reaching demands, and even more important, to pro-actively shape the terrain on which future negotiations of cultural rights take place" (2002:488). Hale and others suggest that, to date, the strategic objectification of "traditional" culture in service of democratic multiculturalism in Guatemala has had dubious effects on many Maya communities (Hale 2002; Little 2004; Velásquez Nimatuj 2005).

The U.S. federal immigration court system may well become another significant site for strategic objectification of "traditional" Maya culture. Hundreds of thousands of Maya peoples fled Guatemala during the Violence. Many of these Mayas ended up in the United States—a few as recognized refugees of political violence, and many others as undocumented workers in the agriculture and meat-processing industries (Loucky and Moors 2000). Writing on the radical Hispanic demographic transformation of the southern United States, Fink provides a perspective that can be used to emphasize the relationship between "traditional" Maya culture and the experiences of vernacular modernities in transnational contexts: "The fact that the 'Guatemalans' were nearly all Highland Maya—people who trace their bloodline and their languages back to the ancient 'corn people' suggested a most dramatic confrontation between the creative destruction of market capitalism and the social organization of one of the hemisphere's oldest cultures" (2003:2). When these diasporic Mayas find themselves seeking legal recognition in the United States, the objectification of "traditional" Maya culture may well be one of the few resources that they may use to explain reasons for their persecution and the violence against them in Guatemala that influenced their precarious flight from the country.

Overall, the multiplicity of language ideologies deployed by Maya scholar-activists, multilingual Maya communities, and powerful social institutions in Guatemala and elsewhere allows us to complicate the work of Bauman and Briggs' inquiry into language ideologies, modernist projects, and social inequality. These ideologies show how constructions of language and tradition may actually function as challenges to new legislators and new forms of exclusion that are produced in local, national, and international contexts. Ultimately, the success of the Maya movement's goals will be affected by the ways in which they creatively incorporate local knowledges and conceptions of modernity into increasingly transnational contexts to further social change in meaningful ways.

Appendix

Transcription Conventions

The following conventions are used in all transcriptions in the text:

: **A colon** separates speakers from their utterances.

Numbers between parentheses indicate the length of a pause in seconds.

[. . .] **An ellipsis between square brackets** indicates that the transcript starts or ends in the middle of further talk.

[   ] **Material in square brackets** is semantically implied in the discourse.

(???) **Parentheses with question marks** indicate unintelligible talk approximately the length of the space between parentheses.

Notes

Preface

1. I have used the actual names of public intellectuals, North American and Guatemalan, involved in Pan-Maya politics. In Miriam's case, I asked her if she wished to be identified by name in the text; she said she did. In instances where consultants were not directly involved in Pan-Maya organizations or activities, I have used pseudonyms and changed identifying information to protect the individual's anonymity.

2. Alarming homicide rates and social cleansing persist in Guatemala due to institutionalized structures of impunity that were not dismantled after the genocide. In this way, the conflict continues to persist in new forms of violence.

Introduction

1. For a complete discussion of the national referendum that included several other constitutional reforms, see Warren (2002).

2. There are numerous erasures entailed in the nationalist binary of Maya-Guatemalan peoplehood. See Cadena (2001) and Casaus Arzú (1992) on discourses of "blackness" and "whiteness." See T. Little-Siebold (2001) and C. Little-Siebold (2001) on diverse local classifications of status, race, class, and color.

3. There are two additional non-Maya minority ethnolinguistic groups in Guatemala: Garífuna, an Afro-Caribbean group with approximately 203 speakers, and Xinka, with approximately eighteen speakers (Richards 2003).

4. Certainly, Maya cultural rights activism has antecedents in the pre-genocide era, as I discuss in chapter 2. Nevertheless, the United Nations–sponsored peace accords provided a heightened and dynamic context in which cultural rights activism burgeoned.

5. Watanabe explains the salient connection between community and local indigenous identity as indelibly linked to "meaningfully bounded social places, rather than institutionally delimited structures (1992:15).

6. The Comisión para el Esclarecimiento Histórico (CEH) found that the K'iche', Kaqchikel, Mam, Q'eqchi', and Ixil linguistic communities were those most affected during the armed conflict (1999:69).

7. "Buscan la mayor autenticidad y tradicionalismo posibles en el plano cultural y el mayor modernismo posible en el plano tecnológico y económico. El movimiento Mayanista es a la vez predominantemente conservador el plano cultural y predominantemente innovador o revolucionario en el plan político y económico. Por ello, se dice que el camino

del movimiento Maya no va solamente a Tikal (tradicionalismo) sino va también a Nueva York y a Tokio (modernismo)."

8. For new perspectives on linguistic practice among Mayas in Guatemala, I encourage the reader to consult the recent works of Reynolds (2002) and Choi (2003).

9. In our sociolinguistic survey, Miriam and I spoke with 128 individuals in the urban center of Chimaltenango, the departmental capital of a Kaqchikel-speaking region close to Guatemala City. Miriam conducted around two-thirds of these interviews, while I carried out the remaining ones. See chapter 4 for a more extensive discussion of my methodology and linguistic ideology as analyst.

Chapter 1

1. The original formatting is preserved to reflect parallel structure used by Maya scholars.

2. As I discuss in "Guatemala: Essentialisms and Cultural Politics" (2008), it is the tension between competing essentialisms—essentialisms with radically different political agendas that share assumptions about the relationship between language and indigenous identity—that situates the particularities of Guatemalan nation building at the center of broader disciplinary debates in anthropology about the theoretical and ethical implications of essentialism.

3. American Indians in the United States have been subjected to parallel processes of state-enforced linguistic assimilation though violence, particularly though the boarding school system imposed on indigenous communities. See Child (1998) for further discussion.

4. "Si la prestación de palabras viene acoplado de opresión social, diglosia inestable/desplazante, y bilingüismo asimétrico, se da el escenario para el linguacidio."

Chapter 2

1. "No queda lugar para una lingüística 'neutra,' 'objetiva,' 'pura,' 'apolítica.' . . . En este país, el lingüista que trabaja sobre idiomas Mayas solo tiene dos opciones: la complicidad activa con el colonialismo y asimilismo lingüísticos vigente, o el activismo a favor de un nuevo ordenamiento lingüístico en el cual se concretice la igualdad de derechos para todos los idiomas, lo que implica igualdad de derecho para las nacionalidades y los pueblos."

2. Taylor discusses how this particular idea emerged as a product of eighteenth-century British empiricism.

3. Stoll notes that the SIL does not "consider itself a mission because its Bible translations, not its members, are responsible for any spiritual growth" (1982:5).

4. Townsend used this grammar as the basis for training other Evangelical linguistic students for missionary work among Native Americans during the summers of 1934 and 1935 when he officially formed the SIL.

5. Townsend uses thirty-two graphemes to represent forty Kaqchikel sounds. What is striking in Townsend's sketch of Kaqchikel phonetics and phonology is the near absence of

linguistic difference, given that Kaqchikel—like all Mayan languages in Guatemala—is the language of the Other. In contrast, there is strong emphasis on linguistic sameness. Much of Townsend's analysis asserts the linguistic similarity of Kaqchikel to both Spanish and English. He informs readers of his grammar, "The alphabet used is as close to that of Spanish as possible" (1961:10). In attempting to use a Spanish orthography to make written Kaqchikel look as much like Spanish as possible, he consistently draws upon similarities between Kaqchikel phonetics and Spanish and English phonetics. Most of Townsend's descriptions of Kaqchikel sounds are, in fact, descriptions of English phonetics. For example, Townsend explains: "The letter a had two sounds: one as in 'father' and the other as in 'along.' Ch is like the English ch as in 'cheese' . . . l, m, n are as in English" (1961:10). Consequently, he misrecognizes sounds in Kaqchikel that do not correspond to Spanish/English sounds and omits sounds that are independently Kaqchikel.

6. Following this same ideology, SIL supported the use of indigenous "vernaculars" in the Americas as instrumental "bridges" to national culture and identity.

7. "La necesidad de hacer una corrección del manuscrito ki-ché para lo cual era conveniente un juego de símbolos genuinamente indígenas para extraer las maravillosas bellezas de la antigua cultura."

8. "Tales dificultades de diverso orden han venido a acentuarse cuando se trata de hacer llegar la alfabetización a los núcleos indígenas monolingües, los cuales habrán de sufrir el paso a un nuevo sistema fonémico y a su consiguiente representación."

9. The alphabets for the four largest Mayan languages had a total of fifty-eight graphemes.

10. "Este instituto quiere también dejar constancia de que se ha ceñido en lo posible a la ciencia lingüística."

11. Other North Americans who worked as linguists with the PLFM included Will Norman, Linda Brown, Linda Munson, and John Dayley (England 2004, personal communication).

12. Linguists worked on several Mayan languages, including K'iche', Kaqchikel, Tz'utujiil, Q'eqchi', Poqomchi', Mam, Awakateko, Ixil, Q'anjob'al, Akateko, Jakalteko, Chuj, and Chorti' (López 1989:53).

13. "Ser un centro de recursos técnicos en lingüística, integrado por hablantes nativos de los diferentes idiomas Mayas, debidamente seleccionados y entrenados. Proveer entrenamiento técnico e intensivo a hablantes nativos de idiomas Mayas respecto al desarrollo de habilidades lingüísticas y educativas, a fin de promover los idiomas dándolos de diccionarios, estructuración sintáctica y proyección cultural."

14. "Necesitamos, entonces, definir y aplicar una política lingüística orientada a la promoción de los idiomas Mayas, no como factor aislado, sino como componente que da identidad, fortaleza y continuidad al Pueblo Maya . . . La información contribuye a este proceso de autodeterminación y específicamente, en cuanto al camino que seguirán los idiomas Mayas, la mayoría de mayahablantes carece de la información necesaria para tomar parte en las decisiones. . . . De esta manera contribuir a que los directamente responsables de los idiomas Mayas, que son los Mayas mismos, tengan los elementos necesarios para hacer valer los derechos lingüísticos."

15. The complete alphabet had sixty-one graphemes.

16. "(1) Todas las letras y combinaciones de letras que indiquen un solo fonema tienen que ser pronunciadas. (2) Cada fonema deber tener su correspondiente forma escrita (letra o combinación de letras. (3) Cada fonema debe ser escrito de una sola manera y no de varias."

17. This publication, the most extensive version produced by the SIL/IIN, presented forty-eight graphemes, representing the Achi of Cubulco, Achi of Rabinal, Awakateko, Kaqchikel, Chorti', Chuj, Itza, Ixil, Popti', Q'anjob'al, Q'eqchi', Mam, Maya-Mopan, Western Poqomam, Poqomchi', K'iche' of Quetzaltenango, K'iche' of Sacapulas, Tz'utuj-iil, Uspanteko, and Caribe.

18. "Lo cual significa que se trata exclusivamente de lingüística aplicada a la labor docente, o sea, sin pretender simbolizar sutilezas de enunciación que sólo pueden interesar a la investigación rigurosamente científica."

19. The IIN organized the Congreso to continue pursuing the same state interest in linguistic analysis that was established in the First Congress in 1949. It also sought to reflect upon *indígenismo* in Guatemala and elsewhere in the Americas (Ministero de Educación 1985).

20. In addition to IIN officials, the organizing commission was made up of several other governmental officials from agencies including the Institute of Anthropology and History, the Fine Arts Council, and the Ministry of Defense. The committee was advised by a specially appointed advisory committee that included Wesley Collins of the SIL, Stephen Elliot of CIRMA, Guillermina Herrera of the URL, Adrián Chávez of the ALMK, and Narciso Cojtí of the PLFM.

21. The academy was charged with the responsibility of "promoting knowledge and diffusion of Mayan languages through research, planning, and programming and executing linguistic literary, educational and cultural projects" (Skinner-Klée 1995:160).

22. "La creación de la academia de las Lenguas Mayas integrada por lingüistas, especialmente hablantes de idiomas mayas. Dicha academia tendría que estudiar detalladamente los factores lingüísticos, pedagógicos y otros aspectos de los alfabetos propuestos para cada idioma."

23. In my interviews, I found that it seemed difficult for linguists involved to provide much further detail about this conflict. They most often shifted our conversations to contemporary debates dealing with other aspects of the language standardization polemic. I take up an example in the following chapter.

24. I thank an anonymous reviewer for drawing attention to this point and its connection to SIL.

25. Maya linguists requested that SIL be prohibited from working on Mayan languages. My visit to the SIL compound in Guatemala City during the spring of 1998 found only a handful of missionary linguists and their families in residence.

26. "Los idiomas mayas son testimonios de la voluntad de ser y seguir siendo un Pueblo, por parte de los mayas actuales. Se han mantendio relativamente fuertes a pesar que sus hablantes no disponen hasta el momento de vigorosos programas educativos que propicien

su desarrollo cultural y lingüístico. Sin embargo, los nuevos tiempos que está empezando a vivir Guatemala, particularmente el planteamiento del Derecho . . . Derechos que beneficiarán particularmente a las nuevas generaciones de mayas guatemaltecos."

Chapter 3

1. Although Max Weinreich is cited by several scholars of language, including Chomsky, an extensive search conducted by participants featured on the online resource Linguist List did not find the passage in written form. See *Linguist List* 8 (306), March 1997 at http://listserv.linguistlist.org/cgi-bin/wa?A2=ind9703A&L=linguist&P=R1482.

2. As we will see, England does not recognize Achi as a distinct language and therefore lists twenty Mayan languages in Guatemala.

3. As of 2001, the play was still performed in Rabinal.

4. This orientation is also evidenced by the fact that to be a representative of the ALMG, one must be a "native speaker" but need not have any formal training in linguistics.

5. "Causo sorpresa el ver que no aparecía el Achi como idioma maya. La Dra. England explicó que el Achi era una variante del Ki'chee' por esa razón no aparecía clasificado como idioma aparte. Por esta apenas iniciando el curso de lingüística, la autora no entendía exactamente las razonas, porque ciertamente entendía a las personas hablantes del K'ichee', pero había diferencias, sobre todo a nivel léxico."

6. "La autora alegaba el derecho de que el Achi sea tomado como idioma; eso se hizo por cuestión de sentimientos porque se sentía que se perdía parte de la identidad cultural como Achi."

7. Nikte's morphological analysis also mentions variation in independent personal pronouns between K'iche' and Achi and underscores that there are additional pronoun differences within them. These linguistic facts invite empirical discourse-centered data collection and analysis.

Chapter 4

1. This point certainly raises more questions about the inclusiveness of the Maya movement relative to other ethnolinguistic groups developing expertise in Guatemala. In recent years, K'iche', Q'anjob'al, and Mam scholar/activists have become increasingly visible in leadership roles.

2. In earlier analyses, I have referred to this construct as the "traditional past," as it was a too familiar binary in anthropological scholarship. Here, I follow Carol Smith's (1996) use of "premodern" to name Maya ideologies that are opposed to "modern" nationalist ones. I include the terms "premodern" and "modern" in quotation marks here to point out that they are analytic concepts rather than ethnographic facts, though quotation marks are not used throughout the chapter.

3. There were no respondents from the municipios of Santa Apolonia, Acateanango, Itzapa, or Parramos.

4. I observed this pattern numerous times in the course of my fieldwork, even among Pan-Maya professionals working in Maya NGOs.

5. In a few instances, an interview subject had both Kaqchikel and K'iche' in their family history. In those cases, I have characterized each individual in terms of which language became the dominant language of his or her family.

6. Maya women between the ages of thirty and fifty-five elaborated most explicitly on the discourses of the premodern past/modern present, although men around the same age also participated extensively in the production of these discourses. I take up the gendered aspect of this discussion in the following chapter.

7. I interpret the "we" in this example as referring to a "we" that includes young, Spanish-speaking urban Kaqchikel women because this speaker was talking to Miriam. This shows her desire to identify with a group of women of which she is not a member, because she is from an older generation and could easily have a child Miriam's age.

8. In Guatemala, this title is highly prestigious and quite rare, given that so few Guatemalans ever complete the five-year program.

9. Severo Martínez Peláez, Guatemalan Marxist historian, also articulates this position as he theorizes about transformations in "Indian" culture due to economic liberation that may be brought about by successful class struggle:

Spontaneously the [indigenous] languages will be abandoned when the "Indians," put in the predicament of conquest or to consolidate a more advantageous economic and social position, will experience the urgent necessity to equip their intellect with the indispensable elements of knowledge in the system and will verify, in the course of events, that it is absurd to hope that said knowledge will be translated into 20 narrow languages with very little diffusion. . . . All of the modern developments, including those that we cannot predict, demand the idiomatic unification of the Indians. (1970:608–9)

10. People who actively want to identify themselves as Ladinos disavow themselves of any aspect of culture associated with "Indians."

11. For an extensive discussion of the semiotics and ideologies of indigenous dress for Maya women, see Otzoy (1992 and 1996).

12. Part of the reason for the distinction between Mayan language and Maya clothing may lie in the expense of wearing Maya clothes, as Miriam astutely posited. Given that Maya clothes are generally much more expensive than Western clothes, to dress well in Maya clothes publicly demonstrates one's superior economic status.

13. One possibility is that the discourse of culture may gradually replace the discourse of progress and its associated language ideologies. The possibility exists that Mayas might successfully reverse language shift while participating in "modern" life. One instance of an incipient reversal is discernible in the Poqomam community of Palín. According to Benito Pérez (2000), Pan-Maya efforts seem to have reversed the process of language shift in Palín, where Mayan languages are increasingly valued as a fundamental part of Maya culture. This reversal is linked to changes in the educational system in a community where Mayas are opening private *escuelas mayas* (Maya schools).

Chapter 5

1. In fact, many Mayan women with whom I've spoken talk about a father's or husband's decision that the family must speak only in Spanish. See the previous chapter for an example of this male role in the memory of one of our respondents. In a survey of Kaqchikel families from Comalapa, Garzon (1998b) found that several bilingual girls reported that their fathers spoke to them in Spanish.

2. Carol Smith argues that in post-colonial multiethnic societies, "more often than not, women bear the burden of displaying the identifying symbols of their ethnic identity to the outside world. . . . Men of the same ethnic group, especially when filling lower-order positions in the local division of labor, usually appear indistinguishable from men of a different ethnicity but in similar class positions" (1996:50). This link between gender and traditional ethnic identity is echoed in the popular notion throughout Latin America that women are "more Indian" than men because of their marked semiotic differences, particularly in language and dress (Friedlander 1975; Rosenbaum 1993; Warren 1998; Cadena 1995).

3. I did not collect any data that attempted to measure actual levels of bilingualism, since my analytic focus was on metalinguistic discourse and not linguistic practice. Assessing the relationship between self-reporting and grammatical competency requires a dual language proficiency instrument. A dual language proficiency instrument, however, does not assess competence in performance.

4. Age was the other most salient factor in individuals' reported bilingualism in Spanish and Kaqchikel and/or monolingualism in Spanish. Age exhibited a metaphorical "stair-step" pattern when correlated with a reported shift from bilingualism in Spanish and a Mayan language, most often Kaqchikel, to monolingualism in Spanish. The percentage of expressed bilingualism (in Spanish and a Mayan language) to monolingualism (in Spanish) generally increases every ten years in the sample population.

5. Farber suggests that women in San Martín under-reported their use of Spanish for these reasons. Richards' (1998) research in San Marcos La Laguna in Sololá indicates a similar trend.

Chapter 6

1. As several scholars have pointed out, access to these kinds of educational and economic opportunities becomes particularly important for women and children who are the most disadvantaged in the global spread of late capitalism (Stephens 1995; Nash 2001; Reynolds 2002).

2. It is worth noting that these spellings are older versions based upon SIL orthographies that predate those used by the ALMG.

References

Abu-Lughod, Lila. 1992. *Writing Women's Worlds: Bedouins Stories*. Berkeley: University of California Press.

Aikio, Marjut. 1992. Are Women Innovators in the Shift to a Second Language? A Case Study of Reindeer Sámi Women and Men. *International Journal of the Sociology of Language* 94: 43–61.

Anderson, Benedict. [1983] 1991. *Imagined Communities: Reflections on the Origin and Spread of Nationalism*. London: Verso.

Bauman, Richard, and Charles Briggs. 2000. Language Philosophy as Language Ideology: John Locke and Johann Gottfried Herder. In *Regimes of Language: Ideologies, Polities, and Identities*, ed. Paul Kroskrity, pp. 139–204. Santa Fe: School of American Research Press.

———. 2003. *Voices of Modernity: Language Ideologies and the Politics of Exclusion*. Cambridge: Cambridge University Press.

Benito Pérez, José Gonzalo (Waykan). 2000. Rescate lingüístico como afirmación de identidad: El Poqomam de Palín. Paper presented at the Latin American Studies Association meetings, Miami, Florida, March 16–18.

Bhabha, Homi. 1992. *Nation and Narration*. New York: Routledge.

Blommaert, Jan. 1999. The Debate Is Open. In *Language Ideological Debates*, ed. Jan Blommaert, pp. 1–38. Berlin and New York: Mouton de Gruyter.

Blommaert, Jan, and Jeff Verschueren. 1998. The Role of Language in European Nationalist Ideologies. In *Language Ideologies: Practice and Theory*, ed. Bambi B. Schieffelin, Kathryn A. Woolard, and Paul V. Kroskrity, pp. 189–210. Oxford: Oxford University Press.

Boas, Franz. 1889. On Alternating Sounds. *American Anthropologist* 2: 47–53.

———. [1911] 1966. Introduction. In *Handbook of American Indian Languages by Franz Boas and Indian Linguistic Families North of Mexico by J. W. Powell*, ed. Preston Holder, pp. 1–79. Lincoln: University of Nebraska Press.

Bokhorst-Heng, Wendy. 1999. Singapore's Speak Mandarin Campaign: Language Ideological Debates in the Imagining of the Nation. In *Language Ideological Debates*, ed. Jan Blommaert, pp. 235–266. Berlin and New York: Mouton de Gruyter.

Bourdieu, Pierre. 1991. *Language and Symbolic Power*. Cambridge, MA: Harvard University Press.

Bricker, Victoria. 1973. *Ritual Humor in Highland Chiapas*. Austin: University of Texas Press.

Briggs, Charles. 1986. *Learning How to Ask: A Sociolinguistic Appraisal of the Role of the Interview in Social Science Research.* Cambridge, UK: Cambridge University Press.

———. 1989. *Competence in Performance: The Creativity of Tradition in Mexicano Verbal Art.* Philadelphia: University of Pennsylvania Press.

———. 1996. The Politics of Discursive Authority in Research on the "Invention of Tradition." *Cultural Anthropology* 11(4): 435–469.

Brintnall, Douglas E. 1979. *Revolt against the Dead: The Modernization of a Mayan Community in the Highlands of Guatemala.* New York: Gordon and Breach.

Brody, Jill. 1986. Repetition as a Rhetorical and Conversational Device in Tojolab'al (Mayan). *International Journal of American Linguistics* 52(3): 255–274.

———. 1991. Indirection and the Negotiation of Self in Everyday Tojolob'al Women's Conversation. *Journal of Linguistic Anthropology,* 1(1): 78–96.

Brody, Michal. 2004. The Fixed Word, the Moving Tongue: Variation in Written Yucatec Maya and the Meandering Evolution toward Unified Norms. Ph.D. dissertation, Department of Linguistics, University of Texas at Austin.

Brown, Penelope. 1993. Gender, Politeness, and Confrontation in Tenejapa. In *Gender and Conversational Interaction,* ed. Deborah Tannen, pp. 144–164 New York: Oxford University Press.

Brown, Robert McKenna. 1991. Language Maintenance and Shift in Four Guatemalan Communities. Ph.D. dissertation, Latin American Studies, Tulane University.

———. 1998. Mayan Language Revitalization in Guatemala. In *The Life of Our Language: Kaqchikel Maya Maintenance, Shift and Revitalization,* ed. Susan Garzon, R. McKenna Brown, Julie Becker Richards, and Wuqu' Ajpub', pp. 155–170. Austin: University of Texas Press.

Bucholtz, Mary. 2003. Sociolinguistic Nostalgia and the Authentication of Identity. *Sociolinguistics* 7(3): 398–416.

Bunzel, Ruth. [1952] 1959. *Chichicastenango: A Guatemalan Village.* Seattle: University of Washington Press.

Burke, Kenneth. 1966. *Language as Symbolic Action: Essays on Life, Literature, and Method.* Berkeley: University of California Press.

Cadena, Marisol de la. 1995. Women Are More Indian: Ethnicity and Gender in a Community near Cuzco. In *Ethnicity, Markets, and Migration in the Andes,* ed. Brooke Larson and Olivia Harris, pp. 329–348. Durham: Duke University Press.

———. 2001. Comments: Ambiguity and Contradiction in the Analysis of Race and the State. *Journal of Latin American Anthropology* 6(2): 252–266.

Carmack, Robert, ed. 1988. *Harvest of Violence: The Maya Indians and the Guatemalan Crisis.* Norman: University of Oklahoma Press.

Casa Alianza. 2000. Casa Alianza Guatemala, Childhood and Adolescence: Basic Data.

Casaus Arzú, Marta. 1992. *Guatemala: Linaje y racismo.* Costa Rica: FLASCO (Facultad Latinoamericana de Ciencias Sociales).

Chávez, Adrián I. 1985. Academia de la Lengua Maya Kí-ché. In *Informe del Congreso Lingüístico Nacional.* Guatemala: Ministerio de Educación.

Child, Brenda. 1998. *Boarding School Lessons: American Indian Families, 1900–1940*. Lincoln, Nebraska: University of Nebraska Press.

Choi, Jinsook. 2003. Language Choice and Language Ideology in a Bilingual Community: The Politics of Identity in Guatemala. Ph.D. dissertation, Department of Anthropology, SUNY Albany.

Church, Clarence, and Katherine Church. 1961. The Jacaltec Noun Phrase: In *Mayan Studies I*, ed. Benjamin Elson, pp. 159–170. Norman, Oklahoma: Summer Institute of Linguistics.

Cojtí Cuxil, Demetrio. 1990. Lingüística e idiomas Mayas en Guatemala. In *Lecturas sobre la lingüística Maya*, ed. Nora C. England and Stephen Elliot, pp. 1–26. Vermont: Plumsock Mesoamerican Studies.

——. 1991. *La configuración del pensamiento politico del pueblo Maya*. Quetzaltenango, Guatemala: Talleres de El Estúdiante.

——. 1994. *Políticas para la reivindicación de los Mayas de hoy*. Guatemala: Cholsamaj.

——. 1995. *Políticas para la reivindicación de los Mayas de hoy (2a parte)*. Guatemala: Cholsamaj.

——. 1997. *(Waqi' Q'anil) Ri Maya' Moloj pa Iximulew: El movimiento Maya (en Guatemala)*. Guatemala: Editorial Cholsamaj.

Cojtí Narcario, Narciso. 1988. *Mapa de los Idiomas de Guatemala y Belice*. Guatemala: Piedra Santa.

Comisión para el Esclarecimiento Histórico (CEH). 1999. *Guatemala: Memory of Silence*, vols. 1–12. Guatemala City: United Nations.

Congreso de la República de Guatemala. 2003. Decreto Numero 19–2003 Ley de Idiomas Nacionales.

Consejo de Organizaciones Mayas de Guatemala (COMG). 1991. *Rujunamil Ri Mayab' Amaq' (Derechos específicos del Pueblo Maya)*. Guatemala: Cholsamaj.

Delgaty, Colin C. 1961. Tzotzil Verb Phrase Structure. In *Mayan Studies I*, ed. Benjamin Elson, pp. 83–122. Norman, OK: Summer Institute of Linguistics.

DeVotta, Neil. 2004. *Blowback: Linguistic Nationalism, Institutional Decay, and Ethnic Conflict in Sri Lanka*. Stanford: Stanford University Press.

Domínguez, Virginia. 1989. *People and Subject, People as Object: Selfhood and Peoplehood in Contemporary Israel*. Madison: University of Wisconsin Press.

Domínguez, Virginia, with Sasha Su-Ling Welland. 1998. Introduction: Cultural(ist) Articulations of National(ist) Stakes. In *From Beijing to Port Moresby: The Politics of National Identity in Cultural Policies*, ed. Virginia R. Domínguez and David Y. H. Wu, pp. 1–34. Amsterdam: Gordon and Breach Publishers.

Dorian, Nancy C. 1981. *Language Death: The Life Cycle of Scottish Gaelic Dialect*. Philadelphia: University of Pennsylvania Press.

——. 1989. *Investigating Obsolescence: Studies in Language Contraction and Death*. Cambridge: Cambridge University Press.

Eckert, Penelope, and Sally McConnell-Ginet. 1992. Think Practically and Look Locally: Language and Gender as Community-Based Practice. *Annual Review of Anthropology* 21: 461–490.

Eisenstadt, S. N. 2001. Multiple Modernities. *Daedalus* 29(1): 1–29.

Elliott, Ray. 1961. Ixil (Mayan) Clause Structure. In *Mayan Studies I*, ed. Benjamin Elson, pp. 129–142. Norman, OK: Summer Institute of Linguistics.

England, Nora C. 1995. Linguistics and Indigenous American Languages: Mayan Examples. *Journal of Latin American Anthropology* 1(1): 122–149.

——. 1996. The Role of Language Standardization in Revitalization. In *Maya Cultural Activism in Guatemala*, ed. Edward F. Fischer and R. McKenna Brown, pp. 178–194. Austin: University of Texas Press.

——. 1998. Mayan Efforts toward Language Preservation. In *Endangered Languages, Current Issues and Future Prospects*, ed. Leonore A Grenoble and Lindsay J. Whaley, pp. 99–116. Cambridge: Cambridge University Press.

——. 2003. Mayan Language Revival and Revitalization Politics: Linguists and Linguistic Ideologies. *American Anthropologist* 105(4): 733–743.

England, Nora C., and Stephen R. Elliot, eds. 1990. *Lecturas sobre la lingüística maya*. Guatemala:CIRMA (Centro de Investigaciones Regionales de Mesoamérica).

Errington, Frederick, and Deborah Gewertz. 1996. The Individuation of Tradition in a Papua New Guinean Modernity. *American Anthropologist* 91(1): 114–126.

Errington, Joseph. 2000. Indonesian(s) Authority. In *Regimes of Language: Ideologies, Polities, and Identities*, ed. Paul V. Kroskrity, pp. 205–228. Santa Fe, NM: School of American Research Press.

——. 2001. Colonial Linguistics. In *Annual Review of Anthropology*, pp. 19–39. Palo Alto, CA: Annual Reviews Incorporated.

Farber, Anne. 1978. Language Choice and Problems of Identity in a Highland Maya Town. Ph.D. dissertation, Department of Anthropology, Columbia University.

Fink, Leon. 2003. *The Maya of Morganton: Work and Community in the Nuevo New South*. Chapel Hill: University of North Carolina Press.

Fischer, Edward. 1996. The Pan-Maya Movement in Global and Local Context. Ph.D. dissertation, Department of Anthropology, Tulane University.

Fischer, Edward, and R. McKenna Brown, eds. 1996. *Maya Cultural Activism in Guatemala*. Austin: University of Texas Press.

Fishman, Joshua. 1972. *Language in Sociocultural Change: Essays by Joshua A. Fishman*, ed. Anwar S. Dil. Stanford: Stanford University Press.

Flynn, Patricia. 2002. *Discovering Dominga*. Jaguar House Films.

French, Brigittine M. 1999. Imagining the Nation: Language Ideology and Collective Identity in Contemporary Guatemala. *Language and Communication*. 19: 277–287.

——. 2000. The Symbolic Capital of Social Identities: The Genre of Bargaining in an Urban Guatemalan Market. *Journal of Linguistic Anthropology* 10(2): 155–189.

——. 2003. The Politics of Mayan Linguistics in Guatemala: Native Speakers, Expert Analysts, and the Nation. *Pragmatics* 13(3–4): 483–498.

——. 2008. Guatemala: Essentialisms and Cultural Politics. In *Companion to Latin American Anthropology*, ed. Deborah Poole, pp. 109–127. Malden, MA: Blackwell Publishing.

Friedlander, Judith. 1975. *Being Indian in Hueyapan: A Study of Forced Identity in Contemporary Mexico*. New York: St. Martin's Press.

Gal, Susan. 1979. *Language Shift: Social Determinants of Linguistic Change in Bilingual Austria*. New York: Academic Press.

——. 1984. Peasant Men Can't Get Wives: Language Change and Sex Roles in a Bilingual Community. In *Language in Use: Readings in Sociolinguistics*, ed. John Baugh and Joel Sherzer, pp. 292–304. Englewood Cliffs, NJ: Prentice Hall.

——. 1995. Lost in a Slavic Sea: Linguistic Theories and Expert Knowledge in 19th Century Hungary. *Pragmatics* 5(2): 155–166.

——. 1998. Multiplicity and Contention among Language Ideologies: A Commentary. In *Language Ideologies: Practice and Theory*, ed. Bambi B. Schieffelin, Kathryn A. Woolard, and Paul V. Kroskrity, pp. 317–332. Oxford: Oxford University Press.

Gaonkar, Dilip Parameshwar. 1999. On Alternative Modernities. *Public Culture* 11: 1–18.

García Matzar, Pedro Lolmay, and Pakal B'alam, José Obispo Rodríguez Guaján. 1997. *Rukemik ri Kaqchikel Chi': Gramática Kaqchikel*. Guatemala: Cholsamaj.

Garzon, Susan. 1991. Language Variation and Viability in a Bilingual Mayan Community. Ph.D. dissertation, Department of Anthropology, University of Iowa.

——. 1998a. Indigenous Groups and Their Language Contact Relations. In *The Life of Our Language: Kaqchikel Maya Maintenance, Shift and Revitalization*, ed. Susan Garzon, R. McKenna Brown, Julie Becker Richards, and Wuqu' Ajpub', pp. 9–43. Austin: University of Texas Press.

——. 1998b. Case Study Three: San Juan Comalapa. In *The Life of Our Language: Kaqchikel Maya Maintenance, Shift and Revitalization*, ed. Susan Garzon, R. McKenna Brown, Julie Becker Richards, and Wuqu' Ajpub', pp. 129–154. Austin: University of Texas Press.

Gellner, Ernest. 1983. *On Nations and Nationalism*. Ithaca: Cornell University Press.

Gossen, Gary H. 1974. *Chamulas in the World of the Sun*. Cambridge: Harvard University Press.

Graham, Laura R. 2002. How Should an Indian Speak? Amazonian Indians and the Symbolic Politics of Language in the Global Public Sphere. In *Indigenous Movements, Self-Representation, and the State in Latin America*, ed. Kay B. Warren and Jean E. Jackson, pp. 181–228. Austin: University of Texas Press.

Grandin, Greg. 2004. *The Last Colonial Massacre: Latin American in the Cold War*. Chicago: University of Chicago Press.

Green, Linda. 1999. *Fear as a Way of Life: Mayan Widows in Rural Guatemala*. New York: Columbia University Press.

Hale, Charles R. 1996. Mestizaje, Hybridity and the Cultural Politics of Difference in Post-Revolutionary Central America. *Journal of Latin American Anthropology* 2(1): 34–61.

——. 2002. Does Multiculturalism Menace? Governance, Cultural Rights and the Politics of Identity in Guatemala. *Journal of Latin American Studies* 34: 485–524.

——. 2006. *Más Que Un Indio: Racial Ambivalence and Neoliberal Multiculturalism in Guatemala*. Santa Fe: School of American Research Press.

Handler, Richard. 1988. *Nationalism and the Politics of Culture in Quebec*. Madison: University of Wisconsin Press.

Haviland, John B. 1977. *Gossip, Reputation, and Knowledge in Zinacantan*. Chicago: University of Chicago Press.

Hayden, Robert. 1996. Imagined Communities and Real Victims: Self-Determination and Ethnic Cleansing in Yugoslavia. *American Ethnologist* 23(4): 783–804.

Henne, Marilyn. 1991. Orthographies, Language Planning, and Politics: Reflections of an SIL Literacy Muse. *Notes on Literacy* 65: 1–18.

Hill, Jane H. 1987. Women's Speech in Modern Mexicano. In *Language, Gender, and Sex in Comparative Perspective*, ed. Susan Philips, Susan Steele, and Christine Tanz, pp. 121–162. Cambridge: Cambridge University Press.

———. 1998. "Today There Is No Respect": Nostalgia, "Respect," and Oppositional Discourse in Mexicano (Nahuatl) Language Ideology. In *Language Ideologies: Practice and Theory*, ed. Bambi Schieffelin, Kathryn Woolard, and Paul Kroskrity, pp. 68–86. New York and Oxford: Oxford University Press.

Hinton, Alexander Laban. 2002. Introduction: Genocide and Anthropology. In *Genocide: An Anthropological Reader*, ed. Alexander Laban Hinton, pp. 1–24. Oxford: Blackwell Publishers, Inc.

Hvalkof, Soren, and Peter Aaby. 1981. *Is God an American? An Anthropological Perspective on the Missionary Work of the Summer Institute of Linguistics*. Copenhagen: International Work Group for Indigenous Affairs.

Hymes, Dell. 1962. The Ethnography of Speaking. In *Anthropology and Human Behavior*, ed. T. Gladwin and W. C. Sturtevant, pp. 12–53. Washington, D.C.

———. 1984. Linguistic Problems in Defining the Concept of "Tribe." In *Language in Use*, ed. John Baugh and Joel Sherzer, pp. 7–27. Englewood Cliffs, NJ: Prentice Hall.

Instituto Indigenista Nacional. 1950. *Alfabeto para los cuatro idiomas indígenas mayoritarios de Guatemala: Quiché, Caqchiquel, Mam, and Kekchí*. Guatemala: Editorial del Ministerio de Educación Pública.

———. 1977. *Alfabetos de las lenguas mayances*. Guatemala: Universidad de San Carlos de Guatemala.

Instituto Nacional de Estadística. 2009. IPC Junio de 2009. http://www.ine.gob.gt (accessed June 20, 2009).

Irvine, Judith. 1989. When Talk Isn't Cheap: Language and Political Economy. *American Ethnologist* 16: 248–267.

———. 1996. Language and Community. *Journal of Linguistic Anthropology* 6(2): 123–125.

Irvine, Judith, and Susan Gal. 2000. Language Ideology and Linguistic Differentiation. In *Regimes of Language: Ideologies, Polities, and Identities*, ed. Paul V. Kroskrity, pp. 35–84. Santa Fe: School of American Research Press.

Iximulew. 1996. *Oficialización de los idiomas Mayas: Retos y Perspectivas*. Guatemala: Siglo Veintiuno.

Jaffe, Alexandra. 1999. *Ideologies in Action: Language Politics on Corsica*. Berlin: Mouton De Gruyter.

Kaqchikel Cholchi'. 1995. *Rukemik K'ak'a' Taq Tzij: Criterios para la creación de neologismos en Kaqchikel*. Guatemala: ALMG (Academia de Lenguas Mayas de Guatemala).

Karp, Cindy. 1998. New Governors. *Worldview: The National Peace Corps Association* 11(3): 34–45.

Kaufman, Terrence. 1974. *Idiomas de Mesoamérica*. Guatemala: Editorial Jose de Pineda Ibarra.

Kelleher, William F., Jr. 2003. *The Troubles in Ballybogoin: Memory and Identity in Northern Ireland*. Ann Arbor, MI: University of Michigan Press.

Knauft, Bruce. 2002. Critically Modern: An Introduction. In *Critically Modern: Alternatives, Alterities, Anthropologies*, ed. Bruce Knauft, pp. 1–56. Bloomington: Indiana University Press.

Kroskrity, Paul V. 2000. Regimenting Languages: Language Ideological Perspectives. In *Regimes of Language: Ideologies, Polities, and Identities*, ed. Paul V. Kroskrity, pp. 1–34. Santa Fe: School of American Research Press.

Kulick, Don. 1992. *Language Shift and Cultural Reproduction: Socialization, Self, and Syncretism in a Papua New Guinean Village*. Cambridge: Cambridge University Press.

Labov, William. 1990. The Intersection of Sex and Social Class in the Course of Linguistic Change. *Language Variation and Change* 2(2): 205–254.

Légaré, Evelyn. 1995. Canadian Multiculturalism and Aboriginal People: Negotiating a Place in the Nation. *Identities: Global Studies in Culture and Power* 1(4): 347–366.

Little, Walter E. 2004. *Mayas in the Marketplace: Tourism, Globalization, and Cultural Identity*. Austin: University of Texas Press.

Little-Siebold, Christa. 2001. Beyond the Indian-Ladino Dichotomy: Contested Identities in an Eastern Guatemalan Town. *Journal of Latin American Anthropology* 6(2): 176–197.

Little-Siebold, Todd. 2001. Where Have All the Spaniards Gone? Independent Identities: Ethnicities, Class, and the Emergent National State. *Journal of Latin American Anthropology* 6(2): 106–133.

López Raquec, Margarita. 1989. *Acerca de los idiomas Mayas de Guatemala*. Guatemala: Ministerio de Cultura y Desportes.

Loucky, James, and Marilyn M. Moors, eds. 2000. *The Maya Diaspora: Guatemalan Roots, New American Lives*. Philadelphia: Temple University Press.

Lutz, Christopher. 1984. *Historia sociodemografía de Santiago de Guatemala 1541–1773*. Antigua, Guatemala: CIRMA (Centro de Investigaciones Regionales de Mesoamérica).

Mannheim, Bruce. 1984. Una nación acorralada: Southern Peruvian Quechua Language Planning and Politics in Historical Perspective. *Language in Society* 13: 291–309.

Martínez Peláez, Severo. 1970. *La patria del criollo*. 13th edition. México: Universidad Autónoma de Puebla.

Mateo Toledo, B'alam Eladio. 1999. La cuestión Akateko-Q'anjob'al: Una comparación gramatical. Thesis, Universidad Mariano Gálvez de Guatemala.

Maxwell, Judith. 1996. Prescriptive Grammar and Kaqchikel Revitalization. In *Maya Cultural Activism in Guatemala*, ed. Edward F. Fischer and R. McKenna Brown, pp. 195–207. Austin: University of Texas Press.

Menchú Tum, Rigoberta, with Elisabeth Burgos-Debray. 1983. *I Rigoberta Menchú: An Indian Woman in Guatemala*. London: Verso.

Ministerio de Educación. 1985. *Informe del congreso lingüístico nacional*. Guatemala: Ministerio de Educación.

Montejo, Victor. 1987. *Testimony: Death of a Guatemalan Village*. Connecticut: Curbstone Press.

Nash, June. 2001. *Mayan Visions: The Quest for Autonomy in an Age of Globalization*. New York: Routledge.

Nelson, Diane. 1996. Maya Hackers and the Cyberspatialized Nation-State: Modernity, Ethnostalgia, and a Lizard Queen in Guatemala. *Cultural Anthropology* 11(3): 287–308.

——. 1999. *A Finger in the Wound. Body Politics in Quincentennial Guatemala*. Berkeley: University of California Press.

Ochs, Elinor. 1979. Transcription as Theory. In *Developmental Pragmatics*, ed Elinor Ochs and Bambi Schieffelin, pp. 43–72. New York: Academic Press.

O'Connell, Daniel C., and Sabine Kowal. 2000. Are Transcripts Reproducible? *Pragmatics* 10(2): 247–269.

Otzoy, Irma. 1992. Identidad y trajes mayas. *Mesoamérica* 23 (Junio): 95–112.

——. 1996. Maya Clothing and Identity. In *Maya Cultural Activism in Guatemala*, eds. Edward F. Fischer and R. McKenna Brown, pp. 141–155. Austin: University of Texas Press.

Oxlajuuj Keej Maya' Ajtz'iib'. 1993. *Maya' Chii': Los Idiomas Mayas de Guatemala*. Guatemala: Cholsamaj.

Pedro González, Gaspar. 1992. *La otra cara*. Guatemala: Ministerio de Cultura y Desportes.

Peñalosa, Fernando. 1981. *Introduction to the Sociology of Language*. Rowley, MA: Newbury House Publishers.

Pike, Kenneth. 1947. *Phonemics: A Technique for Reducing Languages to Writing*. Ann Arbor, MI: University of Michigan Press.

——. 1961. Foreword. In *Mayan Studies I*, ed. Benjamin Elson, pp. 3–82. Norman, Oklahoma: Summer Institute of Linguistics.

——. 1982. *Linguistics Concepts: An Introduction to Tagmemics*. Lincoln: University of Nebraska Press.

Powell, Patricia. 1989. *The Use of Cakchiquel in Two Communities: A Sociolinguistic Study of Santa Ana Chimaltenango and San Martín Jilotepeque*. Guatemala: Instituto Lingüístico del Verano.

Reynolds, Jennifer. 1997. Creating Complementary Research Agendas out of Competing Canons: Doing Linguistic Anthropology in Guatemala. Paper presented at the 119th annual meeting of the American Ethnological Society, Seattle, Washington, March 6–9.

——. 2002. Maya Children's Practices of the Imagination: (Dis)playing Childhood and Politics in Guatemala. Ph.D. dissertation, Department of Anthropology, University of California, Los Angeles.

Richards, Julia Becker. 1998. Case Study One: San Marcos La Laguna. In *The Life of Our Language: Kaqchikel Maya Maintenance, Shift and Revitalization*, ed. Susan Garzon, R. McKenna Brown, Julie Becker Richards, and Wuqu' Ajpub', pp. 62–100. Austin: University of Texas Press.

Richards, Julia Becker, and Michael Richards. 1990. *Languages and Communities Encompassed by Guatemala's National Bilingual Education Program*. Guatemala: Ministerio de Educación.

Richards, Michael. 2003. *Atlas Lingüístico de Guatemala*. Guatemala City: Universidad Rafael Landívar.

Rosenbaum, Brenda. 1993. *With Our Heads Bowed: The Dynamics of Gender in a Maya Community*. Albany: Institute for Mesoamerican Studies.

Sanford, Victoria. 2003. *Buried Secrets: Truth and Human Rights in Guatemala*. New York: Palgrave MacMillan.

——. 2008. *From Genocide to Feminicide: Impunity and Human Rights in Twenty-First Century Guatemala*. Journal of Human Rights 7: 104–122.

Saussure, Ferdinand de. [1916] 1959. *A Course in General Linguistics*. Translated by Wade Baskin. New York: McGraw-Hill Book Company.

Schele, Linda, and Nikolai Grube. 1996. The Workshop for Maya on Hieroglyphic Writing. In *Maya Cultural Activism in Guatemala*, ed. Edward Fischer and R. McKenna Brown, pp. 131–140. Austin: University of Texas Press.

Schieffelin, Bambi B., and Rachelle Doucet. 1994. The "Real" Haitian Creole: Ideology, Metalinguistics, and Orthographic Choices. *American Ethnologist* 21(1): 176–200.

Schieffelin, Bambi B., Kathryn A. Woolard, and Paul V. Kroskrity, eds. 1998. *Language Ideologies: Practice and Theory*. Oxford: Oxford University Press.

Schlesinger, Stephen, and Stephen Kinzer. 1999. *Bitter Fruit: The Story of the American Coup in Guatemala*. Cambridge: Harvard University Press and David Rockefeller Center for Latin American Studies.

Silverstein, Michael. 1976. Shifters, Linguistic Categories, and Cultural Description. In *Meaning in Anthropology*, ed. K. H. Basso and H. A. Selby, pp. 11–56. Albuquerque: University of New Mexico Press.

——. 1981. *The Limits of Awareness*. Sociolinguistic Working Paper Number 84. Southwest Education Development Lab, Austin, Texas.

——. 1985. Language and the Culture of Gender: At the Intersection of Structure, Usage, and Ideology. In *Semiotic Mediation: Sociocultural and Psychological Perspectives*, ed. Elizabeth Mertz and Richard J. Parmentier, pp. 219–259. Orlando: Academic Press.

——. 1998. The Uses and Utility of Ideology: A Commentary. In *Language Ideologies: Practice and Theory*, ed. Bambi B. Schieffelin, Kathryn Woolard, and Paul V. Kroskrity, pp. 123–145. New York: Oxford University Press.

Sis Iboy, Nikte' Maria Juliana. 2002. *Ri K'ichee' Jay Ri Achi La E Ka'iib' Chi Ch'ab'al? K'ichee Y Achi dos idiomas diferentes?* Thesis. Guatemala City, Guatemala: Universidad Rafael Landívar.

Skinner-Klée, Jorge. 1995. *Legislación indigenista de Guatemala, segunda edicion*. Mexico: Instituto Indigenista Interamericano.

Smith, Carol A. 1990a. Introduction: Social Relations in Guatemala over Time and Space. In *Guatemalan Indians and the State: 1540 to 1988*, ed. Carol A. Smith, pp. 1–30. Austin: University of Texas Press.

——. 1990b. Origins of the National Question in Guatemala: A Hypothesis. In *Guatemalan Indians and the State 1540–1988*, ed. Carol A. Smith, pp. 72–95. Austin: University of Texas Press.

——. 1996. Race/Class/Gender Ideology in Guatemala: Modern and Pre-Modern Forms. In *Women Out of Place: The Gender of Agency and the Race of Nationality*, ed. Brackette Williams, pp. 50–78. New York: Routledge.

Stephens, Sharon. 1995. Children and the Politics of Culture in "Late Capitalism." In *Children and the Politics of Culture*, ed. Sharon Stephens, pp. 3–48. Princeton: Princeton University Press.

Stoll, David. 1982. *Fishers of Men or Founders of Empire: The Wycliffe Bible Translators in Latin America*. London: Zed Press.

Summer Institute of Linguistics. 2000. A Brief History of the SIL International. http://www.sil.org/sil/history/htm (accessed April 17, 2000).

Tax, Sol. 1937. The Municipios of the Midwestern Highlands of Guatemala. *American Anthropologist* 39: 423–444.

Taylor, Talbot. 1990. Which Is to Be Master? The Institutionalization of Authority in the Science of Language. In *Ideologies of Language*, ed. John E. Joseph and Talbot Taylor, pp. 9–26. London: Routledge.

Tedlock, Dennis, translator. 2003. *Rabinal Achi: A Mayan Drama of War and Sacrifice*. Oxford: Oxford University Press.

Townsend, W. Cameron. 1961. Cakchiquel Grammar. In *Mayan Studies I*, ed. Benjamin Elson, pp. 3–82. Norman, Oklahoma: Summer Institute of Linguistics.

Trubetzkay, N. S. [1939] 1969. *Principles of Phonology*. Berkeley: University of California Press.

Urciuoli, Bonnie. 1996. *Exposing Prejudice: Puerto Rican Experiences of Language, Race, and Class*. Boulder, CO: Westview Press.

Valásquez Nimatuj, Irma Alicia. 2005. Indigenous Peoples, the State and Struggles for Land in Guatemala: Strategies for Survival and Negotiation in the Face of Globalized Inequality. Ph.D. dissertation, Department of Anthropology, University of Texas at Austin.

Van Cott, Donna Lee, ed. 1994. *Indigenous Peoples and Democracy in Latin America*. New York: St. Martin's Press.

Voloshinov, V. N. 1973. *Marxism and the Philosophy of Language*. Cambridge: Harvard University Press.

Warren, Kay B. 1978. *The Symbolism of Subordination: Indian Identity in a Guatemalan Town*. Austin: University of Texas Press.

——. 1998. *Indigenous Movements and Their Critics*. Princeton: Princeton University Press.

——. 2002. Voting against Indigenous Rights in Guatemala: Lessons from the 1999 Referendum. In *Indigenous Movements, Self-Representation, and the State in Latin America*, ed. Kay B. Warren and Jean E. Jackson, pp. 149–180. Austin: University of Texas Press.

Warren, Kay B., and Jean Jackson, eds. 2002. *Indigenous Movements, Self-Representation, and the State in Latin America*. Austin: University of Texas Press.

Watanabe, John M. 1992. *Maya Saints and Souls in a Changing World*. Austin: University of Texas Press.

Weinreich, Uriel. 1968. *Languages in Contact: Findings and Problems*. The Hague: Mouton.

Williams, Raymond. 1977. *Marxism and Literature*. Oxford: Oxford University Press.

Wilson, Richard. 1995. *Maya Resurgence in Guatemala: Q'eqchi' Experiences*. Norman: University of Oklahoma Press.

Woolard, Kathryn. 1998. Introduction: Language Ideology as a Field of Inquiry. In *Language Ideologies: Practice and Theory*, ed. Bambi Schieffelin, Kathryn Woolard, and Paul Kroskrity, pp. 3–47. New York and Oxford: Oxford University Press.

Yashar, Deborah. 2005. *Contesting Citizenship: Indigenous Movements and the Postliberal Challenge in Latin America*. New York: Columbia University Press.

Index

About the Author

Brigittine French earned a Ph.D. in anthropology from the University of Iowa in 2001. She is currently an assistant professor of anthropology at Grinnell College. She began conducting ethnographic and linguistic research among Maya communities in the western Guatemalan highlands in 1992. French's articles have appeared in *Journal of Linguistic Anthropology* (2000), *Pragmatics* (2003), *Journal of Anthropological Research* (2005), and *Journal of Human Rights* (2009), among others. She is currently pursuing related research about the production and circulation of Guatemalan survivors' testimonies in transnational contexts. At the same time, French has developed an anthropological project in the Republic of Ireland that centers on related questions of language, belonging, and identity in the years immediately following the Civil War. French's current interests center around testimonial discourse, the construction of expert knowledge, social memory, nationalisms, and other forms of exclusion in post-conflict contexts.